THE
RYDER
LIONS

BRIAN BELTON

THE
RYDER
LIONS

THE STORY OF
GREAT BRITAIN'S
1957 RYDER CUP
VICTORY

First published in paperback in Great Britain 2007
By Pennant Books
A division of Pennant Publishing Ltd

British Library Cataloguing-in-Publication Data:
A catalogue record for this book is available from
The British Library

ISBN 978-1-906015-03-9

Design & Typeset by Envy Design Ltd

Printed and bound in Great Britain by
Clays Ltd, St Ives plc

Pennant Books Ltd
PO Box 5676,
London W1A 3FB
info.pennantbooks@hotmail.co.uk

Contents

Introduction

I started writing this book on the evening of Saturday, 1 October 1977. That day I had been to Highbury to watch my team (West Ham United) receive a 3–0 thumping at Highbury. Arsenal would finish in fifth place in the old First Division, trailing the Champions, Nottingham Forest, by 12 points. The Hammers were relegated, having accrued one less point than Queens Park Rangers, who lived to fight again. Although the graceful and artistic Irons lost, it was a good day for me, as it was at that match that I met and spoke to Dai Rees, keen Arsenal supporter and victorious Ryder Cup captain of 1957. His generosity and sense of humour was the motivation for and basis of *The Ryder Lions*.

I had an idea that I might get the book published for the 25th anniversary of that great victory (1982). But then my target transformed into 1987, and before I knew where I was it was 2007, half a century since those mighty moments, when British and Irish golf ruled the world. However, this is all good; right now, the Golden Anniversary seems a fine time to celebrate the memory and the achievement.

What follows is the tale of the last all British and Ireland team to win the Ryder Cup, The Ryder Lions. At a time when the United Kingdom was still recovering from the ravages of war, while being an economic outcast within the European community, a massively strong group of American golfers landed in England with the aim of retaining a trophy they had come to see as their own. In the previous Ryder Cup encounters between the USA and their golfing cousins on the other side of the Atlantic, 11 meetings in all since the start of the great event in 1927, the Americans had humbled the men from the British Isles on nine occasions; the Cup had not been out of US hands for almost a quarter of a century.

Around three months after the birth of Nick Faldo in Welwyn Garden City, a seeming raggle-taggle group, drawn from every corner of a battleworn Kingdom and its small neighbouring Republic, that included the young Peter Alliss and Christy O'Connor, awaited the Yank invasion, but not with resignation; the Great Britain and Ireland team had it in their minds to send the greatest golfing power the world had known back across the Ocean as 'losers', a word and a notion that was an anathema to the people of the United States. For the golfing public of the 'Home of the Brave', defeat at the hands of a bunch of 'Lymies' was something close to an impossibility; anything other than victory in the Ryder Cup would be a humiliation.

For all this, over a few days in 1957, the unthinkable happened and one of the great transatlantic sporting confrontations erupted into a seminal moment in the annals of the greens.

However, the event has been all but forgotten in an era when continents rather than nations battle for that same trophy. Now the 'David and Goliath' encounter that was the Ryder Cup is a clash of titans that can literally go either way. But, for all the excitement this elicits, something of the romance of the Ryder Cup changed when Great Britain and Ireland became part of a broader whole.

Each page within the covers of this book recaptures the 'giant-killing' spirit of '57 that created, for a time, a feeling that there was everything to play for. Although Great Britain and Ireland would never again win the Ryder Cup, the 'Lions of Lindrick' had proved a point and the world had heard their roar. But, perhaps more importantly, this book records one of the great sporting triumphs of the 20th century and so brings to life a shining example to everyone who plays or follows golf and those of us inspired by sport in general, demonstrating that we 'can do better' and that all handicaps exist to be overcome.

The Ryder Lions looks back on the days that ran up to the 'Lindrick Miracle', the games that were played over those two days in Yorkshire and the aftermath of the event, including its impact on golf in Britain and America. However, its central focus is an analysis of the careers and lives of the men who competed in that monumental event, because the Ryder Cup of 1957 was made by them and, to understand it, we have to know the stories of the players who were at the centre of it all. It is their diversity of background and style that helps us makes sense of what happened and how it occurred.

Many people have helped in this task, not least Elaine Sherwood, the daughter of Peter Hawkins, a lifelong friend of Dai Rees. There have been long-distance phone calls and internet conversations. Some of those who were most munificent with their time and patient with this strange Englishman asking them to throw their minds back two, three or four decades have sadly passed on and now play the really big greens.

All this, more than anything else, has educated me. The men of '57, Americans, British and Irish, were motivated by more than just hitting a ball with a stick. They each built their own philosophy from golf and adapted it to all other areas of their lives. This was generated by talking and listening to other generations of golfers, not only those that preceded them, for that group told about those who went before, but younger players, right up to those who we know from the most recent Ryder Cups. By tapping into this 'eternal university', centred on a game no one can ever really win, I found a timeframe of golf that was a vast network of, mostly friendly (but not always), interaction, shared knowledge and people devoted to a game that enriches their lives. I hope *The Ryder Lions* is part of this. No sport, no activity can offer more. If we are lucky, we find our place in the field.

CHAPTER ONE

Before the Storm

Following the USA's Ryder Cup victory at Thunderbird Ranch and Country Club, Palm Springs, California, on 6 November 1955, at the closing ceremony, Lord Brabazon of Tara, President of the British PGA, reminiscent of Winston Churchill at his wartime best, claimed, 'We have learned a lot, although we have lost, and we are going back to practise in the streets and on the beaches.'

Not too many Americans paid much attention to this promise, but history records that Brabazon's words had a prophetic quality.

Golf Illustrated (3 October 1957) in their 'News of the Week' announced 'America's Ryder Cup Team Arrives':

The United States Ryder Cup golf team have arrived. They were met by Dai Rees, who leads the British team against them at Lindrick, near Sheffield, this weekend.

On Friday the team were entertained at South Herts Golf Club. They were presented with a plaster cast of Harry Vardon's grip. Before going to the club they laid a wreath on Vardon's grave at Totteridge Church. In the evening the side went to a 'welcoming dinner' at the Mansion House, organised by Mr Rodway Stephens. Sir Cullum Welch, the Lord Mayor of London, and the Sheriffs were present.

On the Saturday the American team left for Lindrick, where they started practice on Sunday. Throughout their trip a fleet of Jaguar cars has been put at their disposal.

In terms of golf, the post-war era was a time when American players made full use of their many advantages to overhaul their opponents and the 1950s was the 'golden age' for the United States in the Ryder Cup. Christy O'Connor looked back on how the US team of 1957 were viewed at the time, recalling that they were perceived as the most stylish US side since the War, possessing a technical swing quality that gave the impression that the great days of American golf of the 1920s era had returned: 'Swingers of the club had come back into their own to replace the less graceful, though effective, hard-hitting sluggers.'

It had been this breed of belligerent bashers that had dominated post-war American golf, but the US team that landed in England at that time between the end of autumn and the beginning of winter was a mixture of golfing sophistication and focused intent that would have presented a challenge to any rival outfit let alone the disparate if determined underdogs that awaited their arrival at Lindrick.

Prior to the first ball of the 1957 Ryder Cup being struck, Henry Longhurst in *Golf Illustrated* (3 October 1957) gave what might now be seen as an evocative picture of golf as the second half of the 20th century got under way. He mused on the difference between American golfers and their counterparts from the British Isles, analysed the professional attitude of the US Ryder Cup team and compared the playing conditions in Britain to those the Americans had probably been used to. He noted 'the tremendous difference in the physique of the average American golfer and those, either amateur or professional, at home'.

He went on,

It must be remembered, however, that the American tournament professional – that is, the kind who earns the points by which alone a man can be chosen – is a dedicated individual. His mission in life is to make as much money as he possibly can in the limited number of years which he will enjoy in which to do it. He is a man in a hurry, a man with a pack of young and up-and-coming wolves running permanently close behind. A trip to Europe may be all very nice but at this stage in his life he is liable to be concentrating more on increasing his bank balance than on broadening his mind.

Furthermore, every kind of golfing judgement and every book of records must show him or any other impartial observer that … a match between the United States and Britain must be, broadly speaking, a pushover for the big battalions.

3

So if some of them in the past have tended, while they take two or three weeks off to come and play in the Ryder Cup match here, to be looking over their shoulders to see which of their unselected rivals have been picking up the $50,000 in the tournaments they themselves have been missing, it has been only natural. And may I say that I write this in positively no derogatory spirit! I write it because I am quite sure that I should feel the same way myself.

They will find the conditions under which we play golf here incredibly humble by comparison with what they are used to at home – though those who are possessed of true golfing intelligence and discrimination will soon suspect that in the purely golfing sense the game here has certain advantages not possessed by their average country club course at home. Lindrick, let me say at once lest I should be thought to be 'putting my foot in it', is precisely the sort of golf club to which I personally should wish to belong, and the course, which winds its way quietly along between the gorse on the common, is the kind of which I personally never tire. Lindrick is to Sheffield what Alwoodley is to Leeds and Ganton is to Scarborough and Huntercombe is to Oxford and, if you like, what Mildenhall is to Cambridge.

Having said which, I must go on record as saying that our American friends, though doubtless too polite to say so, will be somewhat astonished when they see it. Fresh from his success at Tam O'Shanter, where he picked up $50,000 in cash together with an offer of a year's exhibition matches worth a similar sum, the United States Open Champion, Dick Mayer, may well be taken aback at the difference. At Tam O'Shanter, I remember George S. May telling me with pride the last time I was there, 'There are 13 bars.' The glass doors open with a magic ray as you approach them; 'appropriate music', as the brochure puts it, is piped in to every room throughout the day – one result of which is that two years ago they spent $40,000 on two 'quiet rooms' where talking and music are taboo; and there is a telephone on every tee, which is found to be a great convenience, again to quote the brochure, to 'doctors, undertakers and other professional men'.

At Lindrick there were, if I may say so, exactly two lavatories when I made the usual congenial visit to the club a month or two ago and, as for the telephones, there is a coin box in the hall, which is a great convenience to those professional men who are in possession of four pennies with which to get started. As to the members, it will, I am sure, surprise our visitors to know that they are not to be allowed in their clubhouse at all during the course of the match and have voluntarily relegated themselves to a marquee adjacent to the farmyard at the back, where, if I know them – and I like to think I know some of them pretty well – I have not the slightest doubt that they will prove well able to look after themselves.

Nevertheless I cannot help feeling that most of our transatlantic friends may, when they have overcome their first surprise, catch some sort of glimpse of the simplicity of the 'original' golf of which we in this country tend to be so fond. It has none of the outward luxurious trappings with which they are familiar at home and may perhaps have come to take for granted, but deep down it is the real thing – the same irresistible, faintly ludicrous pastime which causes millions of adult men and women to bash at little balls with little sticks in sand dunes, hills, heaths, moors, meadows and plains, and even, as I have seen in many a country myself, in the barren sands of the desert – where there are no telephones, even for undertakers.

The home side of 1957 was fairly strong compared with the visitors that had played at Palm Springs in 1955. Indeed, it was generally agreed that the Great Britain and Ireland team assembled at Lindrick was one of the strongest for years. The side had been selected using a new system. Players scored points for top-20 finishes in all professional stroke-play tournaments that included the Open Championship. Points were then awarded to high finishes in the Dunlop Masters and PGA Match Play events.

The group of men that were thus assembled were surprisingly confident. One of their number, Eric Brown, took as many opportunities as he could to study the American team in practice and he was not overly impressed. Indeed, though he was in a very small minority, Eric thought he and his team-mates had a good chance of beating the Americans. This was a view shared by Dai Rees, who expressed his opinion at a press conference before the match.

Even so, European golfers had watched what seemed to be a never-ending wave of talent emerging on the other side of the Atlantic. Europe was still recovering from the ravages of World War II and there appeared to be very little hope of rising to the challenge posed by American golf. The USA had huge material advantages and the American professionals enjoyed them to the full. Many British professionals were not full-time players but had to combine participating in pro tournaments with working as club and teaching pros.

Bernard Hunt recollected that there were five or six in the home team who were as good as the Americans, but 'the rest weren't. The problem was that we weren't deep enough. Today it's a lot tighter. I would say the Americans could probably pick three teams whereas we could probably pick two.'

According to Max Faulkner, by the 1950s, the US were calling on players that were all part of a regular tour, and they always had the best transport and accommodation: 'It was first class all the way for the Americans ... Some of our fellows had two or three jobs and tried to win the occasional tournament. It was a bit irritating, but we so enjoyed the competition.'

This being the case, a talent gap had grown that seemed to widen at an alarming pace. Britain could not produce the consistent quality and depth to be found in US golf. Players from the British Isles might have had a chance to do well in foursomes and fourball games, where a strong player could compensate for a weaker team-mate, but most of the final-day singles matches in the Ryder Cup were dominated by the USA; Britain, even when reinforced by the Irish, just didn't have enough players with sufficient talent to offer the Americans a fight.

For Jack Burke Jr, the US captain in 1957, the Great Britain and Ireland players only faced the quality America could provide once every two years, they did not regularly compete with the best and thus were unable to improve and achieve the necessary standard to offer any real challenge in the Ryder Cup. According to Burke, in America the best played the best, then, 'every two years, we kicked butt … We just really had the best players in the world at that time … the situation didn't change much over a long period of time.'

America's captain left himself out of the playing team in 1957 and, in doing so, created the impression that he had little doubt that the Ryder Cup was staying in the USA without too much effort. But only he and Ted Kroll had previously played Ryder Cup golf in Britain and, as such, any close observer of the event would have seen Burke's effective deselection of himself as maybe his first tactical error.

However, Burke also said that he at no time took the Great Britain and Ireland side lightly and never felt that the matches were one-sided: 'I played a guy from Ireland and I saw his grip and I'm thinking, "I can beat this guy." Well, I shot 65 and he shot 65 that morning. Then in the afternoon I beat him by one stroke. That was a rough day, and pretty typical. You beat 'em, but not by much, and they never backed down.'

As usual, hopes were high in the Great Britain and Ireland camp, especially as the last time the teams had met in Britain, at Wentworth in 1953, the home side should have won. The 10-man Great Britain and Ireland team of 1957 included seven men who had played four years earlier: Peter Alliss, Eric Brown, Harry Weetman, Bernard Hunt, Harry Bradshaw, Max Faulkner and Dai Rees, their captain. Added to this, many thought that the 1957 side, which was reinforced by Ken Bousfield and Christy O'Connor from the 1955 team and debutant Peter Mills, represented the strongest challenge for decades to the historic dominance of the USA in the Ryder Cup. According to Peter Alliss, the Americans, without the likes of 'Snead, Hogan and Middlecoff, looked a less menacing bunch than usual'.

For all this, for Dai Rees, the Americans nonetheless would be very difficult to beat: 'Doug Ford, Dick Mayer and Lionel Hebert had won Majors that year, while Jack Burke had won two the year before, and Tommy Bolt had shown himself to be fearsome in match-play in 1955 at Thunderbird.'

However, there did seem to be one law for the USA and another for everyone else. Alliss recalled that the Great Britain and Ireland players weren't allowed to have their spouses with them at their hotel but the Americans brought their glamorous wives to Britain, wrapped in mink coats and wearing diamond rings. Alliss saw this attitude as one of a number of examples of the general 'inferiority complex' felt in the home camp.

Harry Weetman's wife Freda was so infuriated by the situation that she declared that Great Britain and Ireland would not beat the USA because the Americans were allowed to have their wives staying with them in the hotel, while the home side were not given this 'privilege'. Christy O'Connor agreed with Mrs Weetman and later said, 'It was absolutely ridiculous to see grown men kiss their loved ones goodnight at the front door of the hotel. The Americans, naturally, thought this was a great joke.'

But it seems that the regulation might have had a positive effect on the home team in the long term. The US innuendo may have given the Great Britain and Ireland players something to prove. According to O'Connor, 'It was there the laughing stopped … the banter exchanged regarding the home-before-midnight British and Irish players and their Cinderella wives turned to repartee of a less frivolous nature when the match resumed for the singles showdown.'

CHAPTER TWO

Skipper Rees

Dai Rees captains the Ryder Cup team. This will be his seventh appearance in the match and his second as captain. Rees, 44, won no home tournament this season. Last year he tied for first place in the *Yorkshire Evening News* Tournament and won the Swiss Open. Other wins include: Match-Play Championship, 1936, 1938, 1949, 1950, 1950 Dunlop Masters; 1955 Daks.

Golf Illustrated – 3 October 1957

Harry Moffitt, the USA PGA president, once stated, 'Dai Rees always draws our crowds. People really do make a special effort to come to see him.'

Few golfers have given themselves with such passion and resolve to the British cause in the Ryder Cup as David James Rees. He was to play in nine Ryder Cups (1937, 1947, 1949,

1951, 1953, 1955, 1957, 1959 and 1961) and was selected for the aborted 1939 Cup.

Having played with Percy Alliss in 1937 and Percy's son Peter in 1953 and 1957, Dai literally bridged two generations of golf. He captained the side in 1955, 1957, 1959 and 1961, and in 1967 he was the non-playing skipper. Dai won seven games, lost ten and tied one in the Ryder Cup – a fine record for a British player in an era when the Britain and Ireland team suffered many heavy defeats. In fact, Dai was one of the few British players of his era to be truly successful in Ryder Cup play against the overall superiority of the USA, and he is a member of a small group of British Ryder Cup team members who were expected to win their singles matches.

Dai also represented Wales in the World Cup in 1956, 1957, 1959, 1960, 1961, 1962 and 1964.

Born on Monday, 31 March 1913 in the coastal town of Fontygary, near Barry, South Wales, little Dai was very small and made a lot of noise; some of those who served under his captaincy might have said he didn't change much as he got older.

Dai grew up immersed in golf. His father was a club professional at The Leys golf course, about six miles from Barry. The Leys at that time was one of the most important golf courses in South Wales (the club no longer exists, having lost its course to requisitioning in 1956). The Rees family lived in the clubhouse and so the course became Dai's playground. At the age of four, Dai's father gave him his first club, a cut-down baffy, a small-headed, steeply lofted wooden club, no longer in use, which was developed from the baffing spoon (wedge).

(The modern equivalent would be the 4-wood.) Quite instinctively, Dai began swinging with a Vardon-like overlapping grip, but quickly adopted the 'two-handed' grip which he then used for the rest of his life.

One of Dai's earliest memories of the game was as a five-year-old watching the club champion practising and being invited to try a putt. To the amazement of the champ, little Dai potted the ball with a club almost twice his height. Not too long after that, the youngster managed to bogey the first hole he ever played. It was clear he had an innate talent.

While still at school, the young Dai started working for his father on Saturdays, sweeping out the club shop and helping to clean clubs and shoes. He knocked a ball about whenever he could.

When Rees Senior became the professional at Brynhill, the family took up residence two miles from the course, so Dai was obliged to do the majority of his practice in a field close to the family home, much to the consternation of the cows that grazed there. During the summer, Dai rose at 5am and was over in the field practising before breakfast and school.

After leaving education, Dai went to work full-time for his dad. But in those days it was the senior assistant who did most of the playing, while Dai was kept busy with mundane work in the shop. There were very few irons that would escape rust at that time and this meant hard work with sandpaper and sweat. Most nights he went to bed with an acing back, sore hands and arms. But he never grumbled, thinking that complaint might lead to his being sent to work outside the golfing environment.

When Dai was a lad, hickory shafts proliferated, and invariably he was occupied with breakages from the weekend between Monday morning and Thursday evening. Then there were clubs to be cleaned and shoes to be polished. Saturday and Sunday meant more solid activity, including some caddying, which, for Dai, was at least an opportunity to get out of the shop.

However, the young man kept up his early-morning practice sessions and, by the time he was 16, he could hold his own with bogey and was able to beat all the members.

When Dai's father moved to Aberdare, where his mother took up the role of stewardess, the family were once more ensconced in a clubhouse, and Dai was able to play a lot more golf, taking every opportunity to get out on the course. The 13th hole soon became one of Dai's favourites. Rees Senior was the club pro at Aberdare from 1938 to 1953.

As soon as time allowed, Dai entered his first amateur tournament. But his application was turned down owing to his father's professional status, which in the minds of the authorities somehow also applied to the younger Rees. He had little alternative but to turn professional straight away, a decision he was never to regret.

In 1931, Dai entered the Assistants' Championship at Hendon. He covered that course twice in 75. He found that a total of 150 was a long way from good enough, and Wally Hammond of Sudbury won with 145. Dai went back to Aberdare feeling chastised but determined to learn from the lesson.

Three years on, he tried again, this time at Wentworth. The

Assistants' Championship was then a match-play event and Dai was beaten three and two by RL Porter in the final after being seven down at the end of the first 18 holes. But his disappointment was tempered with an offer made by officials from the Surbiton Golf Club, who, having noticed his talent, asked him to take up the position of assistant to Jim Coleman. Dai jumped at the chance of moving to London, where he lived with Coleman and his wife, who treated him as a son.

The work at Surbiton was pretty much the same as in Wales – 120 sets of clubs plus the same number of pairs of shoes to look after and the new boy could only practise before starting work. But Coleman was good to his young Welsh charge. Jim's help and encouragement, combined with his own hard work, resulted in Dai improving his skills on an almost daily basis and he was happy, feeling that he was developing his golf and his personal approach to the game.

In 1934, Dai went down to Sandwich where the Open Championship was being played on the Royal St George's links. When he saw the big sand hills, he was tempted to abandon any ambition to play the course and get straight back on the train, having never imagined such awesome dunes existed on golf courses. He beat 80 in each qualifying round, but that was not good enough and Dai had to pack up and leave before the Championship itself began. He walked away from the Royal St George's clubhouse subdued and disconsolate. He went home and later read how Henry Cotton beat all the low-scoring records and ended a long period of American domination by winning the title. However, Dai had learned that most of the players who had qualified were more or less equal to one another in the long game, but the men who got to the top were those who had mastered the short approaches – the chips, the putts and the bunker shots.

Up to the outbreak of World War II, Dai became a regular in the Open and continued to improve and learn.

Dai's first taste of success in tournament play came when he led the qualifiers from the Welsh section for the *News of the World* Match Play tournament (that was to become the Match Play Championship). The prize money was just a few pounds, but it was a significant milestone. He had won at Rhos-on-Sea and that paid his way to Purley Downs in Surrey where the finals were played. The draw seemed to have been unkind to Rees, he was pitted against Alf Perry, who had a strong reputation and would go on to win the Open Championship two years later.

However, Dai defeated Perry, and was rewarded with a meeting with his old rival Wally Hammond, who had beaten him in his first Assistants' Championship. But it was Wally who was defeated this time, and Dai was never able to decide whether he got more pleasure from the success over Perry or getting revenge against Hammond.

In the third round, Dai was beaten by Mark Seymour, a half-brother of Abe Mitchell (who was acknowledged as the greatest striker of a ball in his era). Seymour went on to the final where he was beaten by Percy Alliss.

Dai left Purley Downs satisfied; it had been his first battle with the Seniors, and perhaps it was because of those two wins that he went into the Assistants' Championship in the next three years with more confidence and determination, going on to win the title in 1935 and again in 1936. For a time, some people dubbed the event the 'Dai Rees Benefit'.

At first, Dai's victory of 1935 gave him a great sense of fulfilment. The *Daily Mirror*, who sponsored the event, had inferred that the winner would go to America with the 1935 Ryder Cup team. However, as it turned out, Dai did not make the trip, but the player he defeated in the final, Bill Cox, did. Cox halved his game with the great Horton Smith, but Dai was very disappointed, thinking that perhaps he had lost his chance of ever playing in the Ryder Cup.

Dai developed a style that matched his character: his swing was free and natural, rhythmic and swift. His two-handed grip was extraordinary but, despite this, his hands rested superbly on the club. At a time when even professionals did not learn a standard method, Dai gripped the club with all 10 fingers on the shaft, one of the few great players of modern times to hold a club in this way. There aren't many disadvantages to this grip, particularly as Dai had relatively short fingers, but, towards the pinnacle of his backswing, he allowed the club to slip into the slot between his right thumb and forefinger, so he needed to regrip on the downswing and this might have been the cause of the odd poor shot.

Dai was never to contest the Assistants' Championship after 1936, although he continued to be an assistant. In the autumn of that year, he made the final stages of the *News of the World* tournament at Oxhey, where Ted Ray, the Open Champion of 1912, was the professional. In the 36-hole final, he met Ernest Whitcombe, the elder of the famous Whitcombe brothers.

Whitcombe, playing superb golf, completed the first round in 69, while Dai managed 75. The Welshman went into lunch five down and the popular theory before the final that Dai would be slaughtered seemed to be proving correct, particularly when the first four holes of the afternoon were halved, leaving Dai still five down with 14 to play.

But fortune smiled on Dai at the short 5th in the second round. Whitcombe, the runner-up in the 1924 Open Championship, having the honour, put his tee-shot safely on to the green; Dai's effort landed in the rough at the side. He was looking six down in the face, but he managed to chip right to the edge of the hole to get his three. Dai's opponent, seemingly suffering from shock, took three putts and, instead of being six down, Rees was within four of Whitcombe, and this was the turning-point of the game. That three was one of six Rees got from the 5th to the 13th. He got through the nine holes in 30 strokes to go two up with three to play.

Whitcombe came back like the fighter he was to take the 16th with a birdie three, but Dai halved the last two holes to secure the unofficial title of British Match Play Champion and the £300 prize money, at the tender age of 23, while still an assistant. He was carried shoulder high to the clubhouse, while souvenir hunters raided his caddy-bag to purloin all his golf balls.

(Two years later, he would win the event for a second time, this time beating Ernest Whitcombe's son, Eddie.)

The win meant that Dai was no longer eligible for the Assistants' Competition, but some great players had watched the final, and the likes of JH Taylor and Ted Ray told of how they had rarely seen such a fine battle and thought Rees might do well in the game. How right they were.

In 1937, Dai went close to winning several tournaments and his stroke average gave him the runner-up place in the Vardon Trophy. The following year, he had more successes and also became a full professional, going to Hindhead, the club he was to be attached to throughout World War II, although he saw very little of it until after the years of conflict.

Dai was a splendid putter, particularly in his early years. He admitted that his best days with his putter were between 1933 and 1939. He deployed an effective slicing action that seemed to give him a relaxed precision often missing in his rivals' repertoire. Later in his career, Dai was a very consistent driver and one of the few British players of his day to master the wedge, replicating the soft knee-action of the American players.

Dai's career stretched from the 1930s to the 1960s and he was one of Britain's leading golfers either side of World War II.

The young Rees came over the horizon of golf as abruptly as an unexpected meteorite at a time when players seemed to reach maturity around the age of 30. The diminutive Welshman, at the then relatively early age of 24, was selected for the 1937 Ryder Cup at Southport and Ainsdale, which would be the last Ryder Cup until after the War.

Although Britain lost in 1937 (their first defeat in the UK), Dai had a triumphant debut. In the foursomes, partnering Charles Whitcombe, he faced the strongest of the American pairs, Gene Sarazen and Densmore Shute, both of whom had won the Open Championship. Dai, although nervous, relished the situation and all day played excellently, which was just as well, as Whitcombe was a little shaky. Level as they played the 36th hole, the Americans were fortunate to be given a free drop after Sarazen had hit their second shot through the green. Shute chipped dead for a par but Whitcombe putted up short and left Dai with a nasty putt of around two yards to halve the match. With the great composure of a natural match-player, Dai struck the British ball safely into the hole.

Dai beat the tough Byron Nelson in the singles by three and one, and he would regard that victory as one of the best performances of his career. The weather was terrible, but he played very few poor shots over the two rounds. To halve a foursome and beat Nelson represented a Ryder Cup debut which for most young British golfers would remain just a dream. Of the home players, only Dai and Henry Cotton, who beat Tony Manero, were successful in their singles and the USA won the series 8–4. But, after gaining 1½ points from two games, for the second time in two years, Dai was chaired to the clubhouse.

Not long into his career, Dai had shown his liking for the excitement of match-play. He made eight appearances in the final of the *News of the World* Match Play from 1936 to 1967 and he won the event four times. In his last final of this event, he was 54 years of age. He continued to turn out in the tournament for another two years. During those 30 years, he probably won more tournaments than any other British golfer (with the exception of Henry Cotton).

Dai was a fighter whose best was seen in match-play but, by the time he emerged as a leading player, match-play had become just a small part of the competitive scene. However, he also had a penchant for winning stroke-play events, taking many titles including the *News Chronicle*, Penfold, Dunlop Masters, Daks and Spalding tournaments. He claimed the Open Championships of Ireland, Switzerland, Egypt and Belgium. For all this, he never won a Major but was victorious in four British PGA Championships. Consistently regarded as a main hope of Britain producing an Open Championship winner (he finished in the top dozen twice before World War II), he was runner-up in three Opens, the first time in 1939 when he was equal second at St Andrews. This was as well as any Welshman up to that time had finished in the Open, and he was said to be the best golfer never to have won the Open.

Many good and promising golfers were shattered by the impact of World War II, although Dai was not among them. In September 1939, it seemed to him, ensconced in leafy Surrey, that the War could not have come at a more inconvenient time. Less than a year earlier, Dai had married Eunice Thomas of Mountain Ash, Welsh born and bred like himself, and had just settled down in his job at Hindhead. The long cold winter of 1939–40 brought plenty of snow, so, between the effects of war and weather, very little golf was played, certainly not enough to keep Dai and three assistants. So Dai volunteered for the transport section of the RAF, cycling to Reading to sign up with one of his assistants, Danny Williams (who would go on to fill Dai's father's old job at Aberdare).

At first, life in the RAF was pleasant enough, with ample opportunities to play golf and keep himself in trim. Dai's first posting took him to Blackpool where, thanks to the kindness of members and his old friend Phil Rodgers, the professional, Dai had several games at St Anne's Old Links, where he had won his first Assistants' Championship.

Soon afterwards, Rees had a real piece of luck, a posting to Odiham, about 15 miles from Hindhead, which meant that on the long summer evenings he could often get nine holes in on his home course.

But it wasn't long before he got posted to the Middle East. He didn't know it at the time, but he was to be away from Britain for three years and two months.

At first, Dai was based in Cairo, and for a few weeks he was able to play every afternoon (in the siesta hour) on the Gezira course, where he met an enthusiastic caddie who, after the War, became known internationally as Hassan Hassanein, the Egyptian champion. It was a great loss to the development of African golf when he met an untimely end in 1957 when, in his own home, at the age of 40, a kerosene cook stove exploded as he primed it. Henry Longhurst wrote of him in the *Sunday Times*: 'His playing record must make him unchallengeably the best Oriental golfer in the game's history.'

Dai trained as a driver. He was posted to Alexandria and got stuck in an office. Of course, the officers were always telephoning him, asking him to play golf, which he got so fed up about that he went to his CO and complained that he was there to do a job and not play golf.

As a consequence, Dai was posted to an airfield in the middle of the desert and became the corporal to fellow Welshman Sergeant Peter Hawkins (from Marlborough Road, Newport, whose family also lived in Crosskeys). Hawkins had joined the RAF as a 16-year-old. Born on 30 March 1919, he was six years younger than his corporal and had been commissioned in 1947. Hawkins rose to the rank of squadron leader. Like Dai, Hawkins had a great sense of the ridiculous. He loved *Tom and Jerry* cartoons and often laughed like a drain.

Hawkins played hockey for the RAF and became a selector for the service (almost like being a national selector at the time). His sister, Barbara, played hockey for Wales. Hawkins came from a very poor mining family and didn't learn to drive until after the War, so Dai drove for him. The pair got on well and had lots of fun. At one point, they found themselves inadvertently driving through a minefield, only becoming aware of their predicament after they were stopped and told that the warning tapes had been inexplicably removed.

The last time Hawkins saw Dai was in 1957 when he was stationed in Churchdown near Cheltenham. Dai lived fairly close and the RAF invited him to a mess dinner. Hawkins didn't let on he knew him and it is not certain if the top brass knew Dai only ever made the rank of corporal, but they were all lined up to meet him. However, Dai bypassed all the air vice-marshals, etc. and went straight up to Hawkins and said, 'Hello, Peter.'

Back in North Africa, during the last advance, in the ruins of Benghazi, Dai found a golfing relic – a hickory-shafted spoon. He likened the find to digging up an Egyptian amulet from the first fairway at South Herts. He used that spoon by swinging at all kinds of missiles (except golf balls) and finally broke the shaft while trying to get distance with an empty polish tin.

When the desert campaign ended, Dai was appointed driver to Air-Commodore Harry Broadhurst, Air Officer Commanding the Desert Air Force, and went with him to Malta, Sicily and Italy.

Finally, Dai got a posting home and 28 days' leave, which gave him time for some golf at Hindhead and to see how well the shop had been kept going by his wife and Willie Hughes, who, apart from that wartime spell, would be the professional at Clacton-on-Sea for more than 30 years.

But Dai was soon on the move again; on D-Day plus five, he was in Eindhoven in Holland. His company headquarters was set up in houses adjoining Eindhoven Golf Club, and his billet, suitably enough, was in the professional's house. Dai immediately began to hunt for golf equipment. He didn't need to look for long as the Germans in their rushed retreat had left clubs and balls behind. Whenever he got the chance, he had a knock and was fortunate to have games with a range of people, until the day came when he played with what was to be his most famous partner ever.

While cleaning his billet, Dai was summoned and requested to make himself ready for a few holes of golf with King George VI, who, owing to poor weather, had been obliged to make an unscheduled stop, and wanted a little relaxation. Dai partnered His Majesty against Field-Marshal Montgomery's ADC and General Dempsey's ADC; they covered the first nine holes in 38, with which the King, who was a sound middle-handicap player with a good knowledge of the game, was highly delighted. 'I only wish I could play more often,' he told Dai as he shook his hand before leaving the course.

This wasn't Dai's last encounter with the great and the good. In Field-Marshal Lord Montgomery's book *El Alamein to the River Sangro* (1956), there is a section that tells how Monty played a round with Dai, just before Dai's overseas service concluded.

Dai's return to Britain was timely as his wife was expecting their first child. He left the RAF in November 1945. He was to say of his service experience, 'War is a dirty, unpleasant, tragic business, and for me it had only one consolation. I had met many grand people, for it is hardship and adversity that bring out the best in a man, and to be flung into strangers' company in strange surroundings is to make one realise that our fellow men are not, after all, such bad fellows. It is a pity we have to wait until a war comes along to discover that.'

The winter of Dai's demobilisation was a period of recuperation and regeneration for many other British golfers, but it took many more than a few months to get back into full working order, and, although the Championships were resumed in 1946, British professionals were nowhere near their best form.

In the first Open Championship after World War II, again staged at St Andrews, some of the players turned up still wearing uniform, including the American Lloyd Mangrum, who was with the US Forces stationed in Britain.

In the second round, Dai produced the lowest round of the Championship, a 67. Rees went into the last round level with the great American professional Sam Snead. Unfortunately, he hit his tee-shot at the first against the rails which ran along the right – and went on to take seven on a hole that was a relatively simple par 4. No doubt shaken by this, he three-putted the next two greens and that was that. Dai buckled with a score of 80.

The American professional tournament circuit in the United States had carried on throughout the War years, and it was not surprising that they took the British Open Championship in that first post-war year. Samuel Jackson Snead was the winner, with Johnny Bulla runner-up, as he had been to Dick Burton in 1939, but this time sharing the place with Bobby Locke; Henry Cotton, Charlie Ward, Norman von Nida and Dai Rees shared fourth place.

This experience, and others in the tournaments which followed, convinced Dai that something special in the way of winter training was needed to recover from the long lay-off imposed by the War. Dai approached his old friend Charlie Ward, who had also been in the RAF, and they arranged to spend as much of the winter as they could touring the United States, on the understanding that they shared everything they earned and stayed as long as their earnings lasted. Since the two men made their trip in October and did not come back until March, it is clear that they did not fare too badly, and the experience was invaluable.

Fred Corcoran, head of the United States Professional Golfers' tournament, met Dai and Ward in New York, and throughout their tour Fred could not do enough to help the two Brits. It was Dai's first experience of competitive events in the United States, and he was amazed at the fantastic level of competition. The American professionals were hungry to win. Most of them had never seen a British golfer, and as such Dai and Ward were a continual source of interest on the 'battlefield', as the Americans called the practice ground. They crowded round their visitors, watching them play shots and from time to time volunteered suggestions. In all his travels, Dai had never come across a more helpful bunch of golfers than the American professionals.

During this tour, Dai got his first sight of Ben Hogan, who he had no hesitation in identifying as the best golfer he had ever seen. Hogan had just won his first PGA Championship, and word of Dai's performance in British match-play events had evidently got around, for a match was arranged between Ben and Dai at San Diego. Dai was beaten, and at the end was further impressed by the quality of a man who was to prove himself to be the outstanding golfer of his generation.

Back in England in 1947, Dai was playing in a tournament at Stoke Poges when two officials of the South Herts Club approached him and asked if he would go to Totteridge as their professional. He accepted and left Hindhead to become the successor to the great Harry Vardon, winner of six Open Championships.

For a year, while looking for a house (no easy matter in those post-war days), Dai travelled backwards and forwards between Hindhead and Totteridge, about 50 miles a day. By now, he and Eunice had two daughters, Jennifer and Gillian, and eventually the family settled in Barnet, only a few minutes by road from Dai's shop where he worked alongside his assistant, Steve Thomas, who had been Vardon's assistant. As youngsters, both Jennifer and Gillian were made little clubs by Dai's friend John Letters.

After a decade's hiatus, the Ryder Cup was resumed at Portland, Oregon. British golf had by no means recovered from the devastation of the war years and the visitors were scarcely prepared, in either playing strength or financial resources, for playing the Americans on their own turf. But those who made the trip did their best, although, as Rees had expected, they were soundly beaten. The only British player to avoid defeat was Sam King, who beat Herman Kaiser.

Dai partnered King in the foursomes against Herman Barren and his old rival Byron Nelson. The Americans won after a real battle. In the singles, Dai lost three and one to Jimmy Demaret. Given that he had played so little, Dai was not displeased with his form, and felt that with more competitive play he could get back to his best.

Two years on, the margin of defeat was far from embarrassing at Ganton, near Scarborough. Dai was astounded how much the fairways had been watered, making things easy for the Americans. But after the foursomes the USA were 1–3 down.

Although Dai was not required to play in the foursomes, he had an inspiring victory in the singles. He had a field day, scoring a 65 in the morning and beating Bob Hamilton six and four. Immediately his match was over, Dai ran from one game to another, trying to give his team-mates some moral support. But it was of no avail, for, although Jimmy Adams beat Johnny Palmer two and one, the visitors had turned up the heat on the second day and won six of the eight singles. The United States team – captained by the great Ben Hogan, just recovering from the accident in which he nearly lost his life – kept the Cup.

Dai won the Match Play Championship in 1949 (beating Henry Cotton and Frank Jowle in the finals) and, in 1950, at the Open in Troon, he was in front after 36 holes. After 54 holes, he was still joint leader. He went to the turn in 33 shots in the final round. But he was unable to maintain his form, dropping two strokes on the 10th, and the eventual winner Bobby Locke, and Roberto de Vicenzo passed him.

At Royal Birkdale in 1954, Dai once more came close to winning the Open. After sharing the lead after 36 holes, a par at the last would have tied him with Peter Thomson. At the final hole, he struck a 4-iron beautifully at the flag. As it turned out, the strike had been too good as the ball finished through the back of the green; he took three more shots (taking a five at the par 4) and Thomson won by a single shot. Subsequently, Dai noticed a black scorch mark on his ball and thought that it might have landed on a pebble. But maybe a more important detail was that Dai had been an uncharacteristically nervous starter and only once in that Championship managed to par the 1st – not a difficult par 5 at the time.

Dai was yet again frustrated at Birkdale in 1961. He started the final round with a seven, but concluded strongly with birdies at the 15th, 16th and 18th holes. However, he was once more defeated by a single shot, this time by Arnold Palmer.

Even so, Dai was recognised as the foremost British golfer

when Henry Cotton retired from tournament play in the early 1950s. Like many other men of small stature, Dai developed a physical and mental strength to compensate. He was a powerful and innately aggressive player who had a healthy belief in his own ability.

The Ryder Cups of 1951, 1953 and 1955 were a catalogue of defeat for Dai and the Great Britain and Ireland team, although, due to the quality of his match-play, his results were usually close.

At Wentworth in 1953, the USA won by just one point and Dai, along with many others in British golf, was convinced that the professional game in the UK was still recovering from the damage done by the War, and, as such, Dai and his team-mates approached the next trip to the United States with a certain amount of confidence, not that they could win (because that was considered almost impossible on American soil) but that they could certainly give the USA a run for their money.

Dai was assured of a place on the points table and was looking forward to another trip across the Atlantic, but he was doubly honoured when he learned that the other members of the team had chosen him as their captain. Previously, captains had been appointed by the PGA selectors, but the new procedure was adopted in an effort to promote solidarity within the team.

In 1955, at Thunderbird Ranch, Great Britain and Ireland went into battle full of determination and they gave their rivals the closest match they had yet experienced on their side of the water. In his singles game, Dai was five down to Sam

Snead at lunch but he got back to one down, although, in the end, he was beaten by three and one. The margin of the American victory was 8–4, but, of the visitors' eight defeats, one was suffered on the home green, one at the 35th hole and five at the 34th. Great Britain and Ireland's biggest defeat was enacted only four holes from home. This being the case, Dai felt justified in saying to the press on his team's return from America that they were sure Great Britain and Ireland had the beating of the USA on a British course.

Eric Brown, a Ryder Cup colleague, said on more than one occasion how much he admired Dai, but admitted to often being at variance with him. According to Brown, Dai was not one for keeping the party happy. He saw that Dai got his own way with suggestions and tactics that were not to the liking of some of his team-mates. Looking back on Dai's role in the 1955 Ryder Cup, Brown remembered that the team were told that they all had to play with the British ball. Arthur Lees and John Jacobs as well as Brown refused to do this; they were sure that no advantage was to be gained from playing their own ball in America. But Dai was insistent. Brown saw something of the same attitude in the 1957 Cup.

For Dai, there was no doubt that the victory at Lindrick in October 1957 had been forged two years earlier on the flat mountain-ringed expanse of Thunderbird Ranch, where millionaire golfers lived in luxury and went round the course in mechanical buggies. At Lindrick, the notion of mechanical buggies must have been like science fiction, but nevertheless Dai and his men took Jackie Burke's team for a hell of a ride.

In the late 1950s, Dai became a national celebrity. He was voted the BBC *Sportsview* Sport Personality of the Year (1957), Britain's best-known sports award, before travelling to Japan to represent Wales in the Canada Cup, with David Thomas as his partner. No golfer had won the Sports Personality award before and it would be another 32 years before Nick Faldo would win it; in fact, in the award's 52-year history, Dai and Faldo are the only two golfers to win it.

In 1958, Dai was awarded a CBE for his services to golf, in those days a rare honour for a sportsman. At the time, he was the professional at the South Herts Club. Living in Barnet with his wife and two young daughters, apart from attending golfing functions, dinners and the like, Dai rarely went out during the winter evenings, feeling he was away from his family often enough in the summer and on golf tours. He had a weakness for watching television and was an enthusiastic supporter of Arsenal Football Club; he would often be found running around Highbury Stadium with the Arsenal players when he wanted to get his weight down in the spring, when he'd also eat and drink in strict moderation. Curiously, for a Welshman of his generation, Dai had no interest in rugby.

Dai had a love for fast cars and drove a Mark VIII Jaguar in the late 1950s. He was a fine speaker and a success on television, and he was said to 'handle a press conference like an angel'.

Dai was a regular winner of titles through the 1950s and early 1960s, but in 1959 the USA reclaimed the Ryder Cup and they were to hold on to it until 1985. Lytham in 1961 was to be Dai's last appearance as a player in the Cup. The format was changed to include two series of foursomes over 18 holes on the opening day and two series of singles on the second day. This made the role of a playing captain, as Dai was that year, very difficult. The Americans retained the Cup but Dai, then in his 50th year, went out on a resonant chord, winning three out of four matches. He defeated Jay Hebert and Doug Ford in the singles.

Well into the second half of the 20th century, Dai's golfing adventures continued. In 1967, he once again reached the final of the PGA Match Play Championship, but was beaten by Peter Thomson. Two years later, in his 58th year, he was once more the runner-up; this was 33 years after reaching his first final. During the decades after the War, Dai was so near to the Open title on several occasions and always felt there was no tournament in the world he wanted to win more.

Dai Rees earned a place in the Order of Merit in 1970 and, when the European Tour was established in 1972, he was a member for the first few seasons. Although by then past his best, in 1973, aged over 60, he finished equal second in the Martini tournament, demonstrating the durability of the game he played. Despite its fast pace, he had a swing which was robust enough to tolerate four decades of tournament play. His consummate style was enhanced by his continuing sound physical condition and an all-embracing zest for the game. Whatever the hardships or the obstacles, Dai had a knack of bouncing back, as hungry as ever for the fight. His aptitude to identify reasons for a poor shot was often comical and sometimes exasperating; he was once likened to the Wodehouse character that missed a short putt because of the 'uproar of butterflies in the adjoining meadows'. However, his unwavering self-confidence was an essential aspect of his potency in the game. He was forceful and could be volatile. Dai was also often impatient, but his energetic and bubbly personality overrode all this; he was always active, and an assiduous supporter of the game he added so much to.

Dai played golf all his life and was made an honorary member of the Royal and Ancient in 1976. He was the captain of the PGA in 1967 and 1976.

TOURNAMENTS AND AWARDS

1936 *News of the World* Match Play
1938 *News of the World* Match Play
1946 Spalding
1948 Irish Open
1949 *News of the World* Match Play
1950 *News of the World* Match Play
1951 New South Wales Open
1953 Daks
1954 Belgian Open Spalding
1955 Vardon Trophy
1956 Swiss Open
1959 Vardon Trophy, PGA Championship, Swiss Open
1962 Dunlop Masters

TOP-20 FINISHES IN THE OPEN
2nd   1961
2nd= 1953, 1954
3rd= 1950
4th= 1946
9th= 1959, 1960
11th   1936
12th   1939
12th= 1951
13th= 1938, 1956
14th= 1958
15th= 1948

Dai crashed his car on the way home from an Arsenal match. Sadly, he never fully recovered from the trauma and died a few months later on 10 September 1983. He was one of Wales' finest ever sportspersons. He was amongst the greatest golfers the Principality has ever produced and he was a Ryder Cup hero.

CHAPTER THREE

Battle Lines

The chronicles of British sport, much like the broader history of the British Isles, testify that the people of the United Kingdom and Ireland are nothing if not determined. The English, Scottish, Irish and Welsh golfers that came together at Lindrick in 1957 were typical in this respect, and they were a bit more ready for their visiting American counterparts than usual. For all this, the US PGA had no expectations of losing the Ryder Cup; they even renewed the insurance coverage on the trophy prior to the US team leaving America in 1957.

On 25 July 1957, *Golf Illustrated* looked forward to the coming fray:

Dai Rees, of South Herts, is Britain's Ryder Cup captain for the second time. Rees was captain two years ago, when the British team achieved the best performance of any side visiting America, and he will now have the opportunity to fulfil on British soil the hopes of victory he entertained on that occasion. So far eight of the other nine members are known.

They are: Peter Alliss (Parkstone) (26), Ken Bousfield (Coombe Hill) (35), Harry Bradshaw (Portmarnock) (43), Eric Brown (Buchanan Castle) (32), Max Faulkner (Selsey) (40), Bernard Hunt (Hartsbourne) (27), Christy O'Connor (Bundoran) (30) and Harry Weetman (Selsdon Park) (36).

The tenth place in the side will be filled by the winner of the Match Play Championship next September, if not already among the nine already chosen, or Peter Mills (Pinner Hill), who is 26.

The nine Ryder Cup players, together with Mills, will represent the professionals in the annual match against the amateurs at Lindrick on August 2nd and 3rd, under the non-playing captaincy of Tom Jones (Maesdu), the PGA captain.

The USA Ryder Cup captain that year was Jack Burke Jr. His team did not include a number of top Americans; there was no Sam Snead, and Ben Hogan (the winner of the 1956 Canada Cup, the World Cup to be) had turned down the chance to defend the Cup in England. Cary Middlecoff and Julius Boros had not been selected because they had chosen to play in a lucrative exhibition match instead of competing in the United States PGA Championship. But, when asked if the

American team were the strongest possible, Harry Moffitt, the USA PGA president, said, 'In the opinion of the PGA, yes … That is not, perhaps, the opinion of all our newspapers. Hogan does not play in sufficient tournaments to make the points. Boros broke a leg and was out of the game for a time. Cary Middlecoff perhaps felt he should have been in, but he did not have the points, either.'

However, it is true to say that a US defeat was considered an unlikely proposition, even in Britain, and the American PGA, in fact, put little pressure on its golfing superstars to make the trip across the Atlantic. Despite this, the idea that America's best had failed to find their way to Yorkshire was actually something of a misconception. Despite the absence of so many fine golfers, the USA fielded a powerful team. Certainly, some 'reputations' were missing, but the US invaders of 1957 would have held their own against their predecessors and many of those who succeeded them. Of their number, only Ted Kroll and Fred Hawkins would fail to win at least one of the three Major US tournaments, but the team included six newcomers: Dow Finsterwald, Fred Hawkins, Dick Mayer, Art Wall, Lionel Hebert and Ed Furgol.

Both the American and British PGAs used systems of selection that discriminated against younger players. The British PGA had a rule that a professional could not play for prize money until they had five years' membership behind them, and the US PGA would not allow players who had been members for less than five years to be selected to play in the Ryder Cup. Added to this, if a player had failed to make the last two PGA Championships, they were not eligible for selection. It is a moot point as to which side might have been the more disadvantaged by these rules, but an educated guess is that many more talented Americans might have been up for consideration than was possible for the Great Britain and Ireland side.

After seven consecutive victories, it is fair to say that the USA were justifiably unconcerned about the prospect of defeat, but, just as in Britain following the epoch of Vardon, Braid and JH Taylor, the professional game in America was going through a transition. The previous half decade had seen a slow demise in the proficiency of the likes of Hogan and Snead, but also (using the advantage of hindsight) there was a growing complacency within American golf. This said, the American team seemed to see winning the Ryder Cup as something of a formality, giving the impression that their victory relied on little more than them making the trip to Yorkshire to play. With an unbroken run of seven wins behind them, one could easily have thought they might never lose. Indeed, the US captain more or less claimed that to be the case. In September 1957, shortly after landing at Heathrow Airport, Jack Burke Jr talked about America's past triumphs and said, 'I see no reason to doubt that this match will go the same way.'

Burke brushed aside the idea that the US team might not be such a potent force as its predecessors given the absence of the likes of Middlecoff and Snead, noting that his team was made up of tournament professionals while many of the home players were restricted by club responsibilities.

Peter Alliss recollected a comment Burke made to a

journalist from the *Daily Mail*, saying something to the effect that, 'If the British team comes back and wins this, you can bury me under 10 tons of compost.'

But Burke's attitude might have had an element of bravado. Dow Finsterwald later confessed, 'I was nervous in 1957, and was still nervous in '59 [at Eldorado Country Club, in Palm Springs, California].'

The Great Britain and Ireland team was once more skippered by the warrior-like Dai Rees who had played an inspiring round before leaving for Lindrick, breaking the record for his home course at the South Herts Club, Totteridge. Playing in a challenge round against the club members, he scored 67 to beat the previous record, held by CA Thompson and Ken Bousfield, by one stroke.

Deploying a new system of selection, like the American two-year points list, the Great Britain and Ireland team included one debutant, Peter Mills, to Ryder Cup combat, and the recall of Peter Alliss and Bernard Hunt made the home side, for many, look the strongest ever pitted against the USA in the Ryder Cup.

APPEAL TO THE PRESS

Dai Rees was anxious about press reactions about his team's chances. His experience of the Ryder Cup, and in particular of those played in America, had convinced him that golf writers had a huge influence on events. So, on the last practice day, he asked for an early-morning press conference before he went on to the course. The golf correspondents turned up in force, despite it being held at an unearthly hour for most journos. After Rees had said his piece, the gathered hacks assured him of their support and expressed their confidence in the home side's chances.

Rees had wanted to make a very simple and straightforward point, asking the press to give his team a break and not depict the USA as an invincible force unless they proved themselves to be such. The papers that evening and the following morning carried just the right kind of sober, objective summing-up of Great Britain and Ireland's chances that Rees had hoped for. There were no arrogant boasts about what would be done to the Americans or gloomy forecasts about how the USA would demolish Great Britain and Ireland. Rees was controlling the variables like the skilled general he was.

THE COURSE

Henry Cotton said after the 1955 match that he couldn't visualise a Great Britain and Ireland team winning in America but that there was a chance of their defeating the USA on British soil.

Near the Yorkshire city of Sheffield, Lindrick is an inland course. The Ryder Cup put it on the golfing map, but the Sheffield and District Golf Club, as it was initially called, had been founded back in 1891. The legendary Tom Dunn laid out the first nine holes on Lindrick Common and an additional nine holes were set out in 1894. The club changed its name to Lindrick Golf Club in 1934, and the internationally celebrated golf architect Fred Hawtree, of the renowned British firm Hawtree and Sons, made more modifications to the design of the course.

Lindrick was placed on limestone prime common land and the exceptional turf provided a mixed heathland and moorland ambiance; picturesque but wild, its silver birch-lined fairways, gorse and heather evoke a unique feeling. The fairways are munificent and perfectly conditioned, the greens finely tended, fast and protected by bunkers. Precision, more than length, is crucial when playing the Lindrick course. When the gorse is in bloom in the spring, it's a beautiful venue for golf.

Although some find the start uninspiring, the course improves the further you go round (many players argue that the best holes are across the busy and noisy A57 that divides the course and runs close to a number of the holes). However, the greens at Lindrick encompass a good proportion of tough holes, particularly on the back nine, and the 4th, a short par 5 of 478 yards, is definitely entertaining as well as unforgettable, with a downhill drive and a blind approach to a concealed green, snuggled up in a hollow.

Bernard Darwin, the grandson of the great naturalist Charles Darwin, invented golf writing as we know it today. He was the first golf writer to transcribe facts and figures into a branch of literary journalism and he did so with a witty panache, and an exceptional turn of phrase. In an article for *The Times* (which he wrote for from 1907 to 1953) 'At Hollinwell and Lindrick' (reproduced in his book *Playing the Like*), he wrote of the 'secret and engaging dell' around the 4th green, which at one time bordered three counties: 'York, Notts and Derby – and so it was once the ideal spot for prize-fighting. If there was an obdurate magistrate on one side of the water there was probably a complaisant one on the other, and the ring could be reformed without much ado.'

In a more recent publication, the 18th hole is detailed in *The 500 World's Greatest Golf Holes* (George Peper and Editors of *Golf Magazine*, 2003). It's a 210-yard par 3. It's extraordinary to conclude with a par 3 and slightly malicious to have such a demanding final tee-shot, especially if a game is in the balance.

As is the case with many courses of Lindrick's period, it is not long enough to host contemporary tournaments for men. But, during 1966, it was the venue for the British Masters, which was won by Neil Coles, and Vivien Saunders was victorious in the Women's British Open played there in 1977.

Oddly, in 1982, it took Greg Norman 14 strokes at Lindrick's 17th, a par 4, in the final round of the Martini tournament. He went on to claim victory at St Pierre a few weeks later, in the British Masters, winning by eight strokes.

Lindrick continues to stage significant amateur events and provide a fine challenge to golfers of any handicap, but its crisp turf can test even the best players.

Men planning to visit Lindrick should take a jacket and tie with them if they have plans to eat or drink in the main bar, or they'll be restricted to the Ryder Cup room, which is still OK in terms of quality and atmosphere. Lindrick is a straightforward and affable club that epitomises the conventions and customs of English golf.

Lindrick's well-drained firm fairways provide one of the fastest and truest but at the same time trickiest courses in

England, so good putters love it. The bunkering is a pleasure. The course has a distinguished history and noble tradition.

However, Lindrick was not a popular choice as the venue for the 1957 Ryder Cup. Widely thought of as mainly a heathland course with tree-lined fairways, it was believed to be more of an advantage to the Americans than links courses such as Southport and Ainsdale, as it was similar to the courses that the Americans played on week in, week out. As such, it wasn't seen as the most suitable place to upset the American run of victories. Another disadvantage was that it was twice bisected by a main road. But the main point of criticism was the relative shortness of the course, just 6,541 yards in length, and too short to test the American long hitters. It was said to have too many holes requiring just a drive and wedge. With the US players being the unquestioned masters with short irons, two extra tees were constructed to lengthen the course, but the pressure from the British press for a change of venue continued almost up to the last minute.

In actuality, the British PGA, who accepted Lindrick as the stage for the Ryder Cup, had very limited choice in the matter. Interest in the event was diminishing. Just a few months before the event was due to be played in Britain, worries surfaced that financial backing would not be found. The Ryder Cup was in danger, but was rescued by a last-gasp sponsor: Yorkshire industrialist Sir Stuart Goodwin, the founder of an important Sheffield steel and tool-making firm, Neepsend Ltd., and a man of considerable wealth. As a young man, he had come near to death from diabetes and was saved only by the timely discovery of insulin, of which he was one of the first experimental users. The rest of his life, and that of his wife, Lady Goodwin, was marked by enthusiastic charitable donations to numerous causes in the locality, especially hospitals. The central fountain in Sheffield, boasting 89 individual jets, is dedicated to his and Lady Goodwin's memory and their services to the city.

Stuart Goodwin, although not a golfer himself, had become enthusiastic about the game, and, like Sam Ryder, the founder of the Ryder Cup, had come to golf late in life. He had seen Dai Rees and Fred Daly play an exhibition match at Lindrick and, taken with the skill shown by the two men, the 58-year-old tycoon arranged to meet the Secretary of the British PGA, Commander Roe, to talk about staging a big tournament at Lindrick. A three-year £15,000 sponsorship of a professional tournament was agreed.

Going back to the same well, the British PGA approached Goodwin for funding for the 1957 Ryder Cup. Goodwin agreed to put up £10,000 and promised that the PGA would also receive all the gate money if the match was played at his home club. It was said in some quarters that Dai Rees had been involved in the decision to play the Cup at Lindrick, which would have meant Goodwin had consulted the Welshman at some point. But the course was set up to play hard and fast, almost like a links course, and Rees, who was recognised as an inspirational leader and a brilliant strategist, quite rightly calculated that, although not all his players knew Lindrick well, *he* did, and the Americans had little or no knowledge of the course.

DETAILS OF THE LINDRICK COURSE IN 1957					
Hole	Distance	Distance	Par Hole	Distance	Par
1	400	4	10	374	4
2	358	4	11	170	3
3	164	3	12	460	4
4	472	5	13	470	5
5	400	4	14	516	5
6	138	3	15	351	4
7	427	4	16	486	5
8	318	4	17	387	4
9	436	4	18	200	3
		35			37
				= Par 72 (6,527 yards)	

CHAPTER FOUR

Captain America

Jack Burke, 34, is a worthy man to captain the team, having an unblemished record of six points from the last three matches. He had his best season in 1956 when he won both the Masters' Tournament and the PGA Match-Play Championship. This season he has been troubled with an injured hand.

Golf Illustrated – 3 October 1957

John Joseph 'Jack' Burke Jr was born on 29 January 1923 in Fort Worth, Texas. He was selected for the US Ryder Cup team in 1951, 1953, 1955, 1957 and 1959, and captained the Americans in 1957 and 1973. Jackie won seven of the eight games he played in the Ryder Cup and, as non-playing captain in 1973, lead the USA to victory at Muirfield.

Jackie was the last of eight children and he began playing

golf as a six-year-old. His mother, Quo Vadis Quayle, was raised in Fort Worth where she met Jackie's father, a golf pro from Philadelphia. Having married and started a family, the Burkes moved to Houston where Jack Senior had got a job as golf pro at the River Oaks Country Club, a position he held until he died in 1943. Some of Jackie's earliest golfing memories are of playing golf with his mother at River Oaks; he used a 4-iron to wallop a ball while she played. But during the years of the Depression young Jackie was not allowed in the clubhouse, so he mixed with the caddies who taught him the important rudiments of the game.

In 1920, the elder Burke had tied for second place in the US Open (behind Ted Ray) and was the winner of a number of tournaments. Jack Senior also invented and secured a patent on the first all-weather (cord) grip. Jackie's father instilled an appreciation for the rules of golf in him and taught him the ethic that there was a right way to play the game. These were convictions that Jack Junior held on to throughout his career.

Jack Senior was a good teacher who helped some of the best players of his era, making champions of the likes of Craig Wood, a runner-up in five Major championships before winning the Masters; Henry Picard, who won the 1938 Masters and the 1939 US PGA; Ben Hogan, known as one of the finest golfers who ever lived; Byron Nelson, a five-time national championships winner, and Babe Didrikson (Zaharias) one of the greatest ever women players who, between 1940 and 1955, achieved 41 victories on the LPGA Tour and won 10 Majors. Jack recalled playing a lot with her as a child and that she was strong and mentally tough. He remembers the day he outdrove her as one of the great days of his life. But perhaps the thing he admired most about Babe was that she loved to bet and take risks. Jack saw this as being what made her such a superb practitioner of the game.

When such giants of golf came to Jack Senior for lessons, they constantly talked about the sport; Jack listened to them intently and usually got a lesson before they left. The youngster always enjoyed the hustlers and was adamant that he learned little from the golfers who didn't have 'a little hustle in them'.

For Jack, anyone who has been a caddie has been hustled by the best. Remembering his own time as a caddie, he recollected how the caddies waiting to be hired would be ready for their colleagues who had been successful in getting a bag to return to lure them into using their hard-earned dollars to fuel dice and card games. For Jack, that was his mental training ground and how he learned to know the value of taking a chance.

Burke was appreciative of his father's ability to guide and instruct others and saw him as a marvellous teacher with a great love of the game. But he believes these qualities accompany the achievement of successfully raising eight children and playing an active role in the local and golfing community.

Jack recalled that his dad avoided telling other players outright what they should do, but chose to teach them lessons that they might use throughout their careers using parables. It was a style Jack replicated in his teaching.

Jack recalled that, as a child, he was asthmatic and couldn't run and play like the other kids. So he would sit on the lesson tee at River Oaks Country Club in Houston and watch his father teach. One day, his dad was teaching a player who was having difficulty understanding what Jack Senior was trying to tell him about releasing the club. Young Jack watched as his father instructed his student to throw his clubs down the range as far as he could. The watching youngster got the job of picking the clubs up again and again, but he understood that his father was teaching by actions something that couldn't be taught in words. Jack saw that you can't teach or write a book about how to throw something; it is a skill that has to be demonstrated and self-taught by doing. This means working with a player to swing a club without pressure, not pushing, shoving, directing, wishing or hoping; you just 'swing'.

However, Jack was wise enough to know that this was easy to say but very hard to do. For him, the golf swing relies on trust. He observed that few people trust what they are doing. Thus, it is hard to trust themselves to swing the club correctly, with confidence. He made the point that trust cannot be manufactured just as you can't manufacture a good swing; trust is something that grows within a person as they become more confident in their actions. As such, trust is not so much taught as learned on the basis of repeated practice; it is an aspect of the personality that is developed, nurtured and honed in the corporal environment. For Jack, the golfer who stands on the 1st tee at Augusta or Wentworth and makes a good swing is a player who trusts what they are doing.

Jack Senior hired the young Jimmy Demaret (who in the future would be inducted into the World Golf Hall of Fame) as an assistant pro, and Jim became something of a mentor to the young Jackie. It was the start of a lifelong friendship. As a young man hanging around the River Oaks pro shop, Jackie, along with some caddies, would sneak out on the greens, where they were forbidden to play, and practise. This being the case, he pushed the boundaries from his earliest days.

The Burke household was a meeting place for some of the finest professionals of the 1930s and 1940s including Dick Metz, Jack Grout, Jimmy Thomson and Toney Pana. Jackie would sit and listen to the conversations between these men and the stories told by them and it was through this 'narrative education' that Jackie learned lessons that would hold him in good stead for the rest of his life.

Jackie gave his first golf lesson at the age of 13 and turned professional in 1940 and, before he reached 20, he was working as a pro at Galveston Country Club. However, his father discouraged him from playing professionally. His hands were small, which restricted the power of his swing, but Burke compensated by developing a good touch in his fingers and other skills, such as the ability to judge distance. So, undeterred by parental discouragement, he turned professional and qualified for his first US Open in 1941.

At this point, Jack was a student at Rice University, but he left to join the Marine Corps, where he served as a martial-arts and drill instructor. In 1946, after being mustered out of the service, he became a full-time golfer rather than returning to university. In 1950, he won four times on the PGA Tour.

Given this background, it was not surprising that Jack developed into a top-class golfer. He was at his best in the 1950s, but he also won tournaments early on in the 1960s.

Jack first came to prominence after two victories in the 1951 Ryder Cup. In 1952, he won four consecutive tournaments (equalling the fifth-best such streak in PGA Tour history). This time was marked by his magnificence in the putting aspect of the game, and he was to admit that, during this period, he was putting better than he would at any time during his whole career.

When the streak started he wasn't playing that well, but then he got an Otey Crisman putter from Jay Hebert. His run of brilliance started when he won the Texas Open, finishing with rounds of 64–64 on the same day. He recalled, 'I made everything I looked at.'

Then came the Houston Open and in cold weather Jack made putt after putt. On to Baton Rouge and, although he wasn't hitting the ball that well, he was confident that all he had to do was get the ball somewhere on the green and the putter would do the rest. Jack won again. Then he went to Florida and holed putts from everywhere, many of them fantastic long-distance efforts. He started the last nine holes with a nine-shot lead. He said of this time, 'I could hit any side of the hole from any distance at any time. It wasn't a question of whether I was going to putt well, but how good I was going to putt.'

It seemed everything was going Jack's way. In that same year, he was voted 'the handsomest athlete in America'.

Jack was amongst the finest 'bad-weather' players in golf, as evidenced in the 1952 Masters. The wind was sadistic but his closing round of 69 was the only score under 70 during the last two days. He finished as runner-up to Sam Snead but won the Vardon Trophy for lowest-scoring average that year.

Perhaps Jack's most famous match was a nine-hour, 40-hole quarter-final loss to Cary Middlecoff in the 1955 PGA Championship but he matured as a golfer in 1956, winning two Major championships. The weather at the Masters was again problematic, but Jack made up eight shots, soaring to an 80, in the last round over the 24-year-old amateur Ken Venturi, who had led by four shots. The scores were high that day. Just hitting the greens was a massive challenge. Putting was another trial, as the rain made the grass slick. He recalled being shocked that he won: 'It was just a horrendous day, 40–50 mph winds, cold and dark. It was the worst day you ever saw in your life.'

Jack hit a good drive on the 1st hole and had a 3-wood in for his 2nd (it was usually an 8- or 9-iron). On the 4th, a par 3, he hit a driver and a 9-iron. He was later to say that the pressure that day was 'to not shoot 100'.

Venturi was leading, but he was an amateur and couldn't take any of the money. So Doug Ford and Jack were on the practice green talking about it. Jack remembered telling Ford, 'If somebody can shoot a 75 today, they are going to take home some cash.'

Jack was the only player out of the field of 60 to hold his ball on the 17th green that day, and, for him, 'The win was just unbelievable.'

It was indeed a win that showed fortitude and

determination. Clear evidence of this could be found on that 17th hole where all the sand had been blown out of the bunker and up on the green.

Burke had tightened his putting stance and took smaller strokes using a technique he calls 'tap putting'. On the 17th, he hit a 15-foot putt and claims the wind drove it half the way there. He shot a 71, one under par, which was good under the conditions; in fact, it was the lowest round of the day. Venturi just couldn't make it on the back nine and he handed Jack the trophy. According to Jack, 'I thank him a lot for that.'

Jack won the US PGA Championship when the tournament was a match-play event, edging Ted Kroll, three and two, in the final. At that point, Jack considered that he was at last achieving his potential, and that the weight of his father's expectation had been taken from his shoulders. Looking back on that victory, he reflected on how he beat eight players to win the PGA. He recollected that each day he felt like he was standing on the edge of a cliff and that someone was going to push him off. At no point did he believe he was going to win the PGA.

On the American Tour, Jack won 17 tournaments and was named Player of the Year in 1956. But, for all his success, and even though he was among the top-10 money-winners five times, Jack wasn't making really big bucks and started to withdraw from the Tour.

During the 1950s, Jack was involved in four winning Ryder Cup teams and, alongside Sam Snead, was America's most successful player in that competition, often playing like a genius. In 1953, in his foursomes match with Ted Kroll, the two men completed their morning round in 66 strokes, seven up on Jimmy Adams and Bernard Hunt. In 1955, Jackie partnered Tommy Bolt in a match against Arthur Lees and Harry Weetman; it was one of the most exciting Ryder Cup encounters ever played. The Brits made 68 before lunch which put them one up. During the afternoon, they went out in 34 shots – still only one up. But the Americans pulled in front over the closing holes to beat their opponents with a birdie on the final green.

It was odd that captain Sam Snead failed to give Jack a game in the 1959 Ryder Cup in California.

Jack and Jimmy Demaret had purchased some land in a deserted part of Houston, Texas, in 1957. With the help of architect Ralph Plummer, this would become the Champions Golf Club. They built two courses – Cypress Creek and Jackrabbit. The Cypress Creek course hosted the 1967 Ryder Cup, the 1969 US Open and five Tour Championships were played there. Ben Hogan chose the course to make the final tournament appearance of his career at the 1971 Houston Champions International and, in 2003, it hosted its fifth Tour Championship for the top-30 money-winners on the PGA Tour.

The Burke/Demaret partnership lasted until Jimmy's death in 1983, but to this day Jack continues to gives lessons at Champions.

The father of six children, Jack married his second wife Robin (formerly Moran), a former Texas State Women's Amateur Champion, in 1987. He fathered his youngest child in 1989.

For Jack, to play golf well, there is a need for sensitivity and imagination. He regrets how the will of the Champions membership prevailed, and they painted yardages on the sprinkler heads. He called the moment of that decision the worst day of his life.

Jackie became a teacher of high repute following his departure from the Tour. He has worked with men like Ben Crenshaw, Phil Mickelson and Hal Sutton. In 2004, Burke was Sutton's assistant captain at the Ryder Cup. Another pupil was Steve Elkington, a member of the Champions Club who lived in Houston. When Elkington was asked what inspired him to drop a 15-foot birdie putt to win the 1991 Players Championship, only his second Tour victory, it wasn't the prize money of close to $300,000 or the 10-year PGA Tour exemption. According to Elkington, as he lined up the putt, he thought how Jack, then close to 70 years old, was probably watching how he managed the pressure. According to Elkington, knowing Jack was such a demanding teacher, he understood that he had to make the putt 'or I wouldn't be able to take the heat next week ... When Jackie Burke cares enough to talk to you, you don't want to get caught staring out the window.'

According to Gary Player, 'Whenever anybody needed any help, we would always go to Jackie and say, "Jackie, I'm struggling with my game," and he would help you kindly.'

For Hal Sutton, Jack Burke is 'one of the few people left who really understands this game in its entirety ... He's really current with the game. He's seen all the great players. He knows how they hit it. He understands the golf swing; he's made it happen, and he's been a great player in his own day.'

For Jack, golf is an art, not a science: 'Playing golf is a hobby, and the hobby is not the *act* of hitting a golf ball. I mean, it's no fun hitting 2-irons into a cold wind. It's in the *learning*.'

In this, Jack showed his insight into the nature of sport in general; win or lose, there is no point in it as an end in itself, it is what it does for and to a person that is of worth.

Jack has a favourite story to illustrate his meaning. While visiting a friend's office, he noticed a striking figure of a dog carved out of wood on his desk. On enquiring, Jack found out that his friend had carved it himself. When he asked how he had gone about this task, the carver answered, 'I got a block of wood and a knife and I cut away everything that didn't look like a dog.'

For Jack, that illustrated how to give a lesson. The teacher watches the person swing a golf club and builds up a visual image of what that person's swing should look like. Then the teacher does what they need to do to get the person to swing in a way that fits that image. That, according to Jack, makes the teaching of golf and the game in general an art. The best teachers in any field will recognise this; teaching is not a matter of putting something into a person, this is basically a deficit model of people based on the assumption that the student lacks some element that only the teacher can give. However, learning actually comes about through the means by which a teacher can work with someone to express their potential. This is based on a positive view of humanity that sees individuals as being complete in themselves, but who are able to grow and extend their existing boundaries via the development of awareness and insight.

But perhaps it is Jack's philosophy of putting and his general approach to the playing of golf that best shows his feeling for the finer points of the game. 'It should be as natural as putting your shoes on,' he says.

He has pointed out that, if a player is thinking about where their hands are, how they are standing and all the other considerations that the manuals are full of, that is not going to make you a good putter. Jack's idea is to roll the ball with whatever God gave you and, however you do it, that's what your stroke is. This becomes a kind of discipline in itself, in that you have to feel for it daily. It's a matter of changes and adjustments. Jack's position on putting is that it is like rolling something with your hand except you're using a stick; every putt is straight. This understanding together with grasping that the ball is the thing that breaks and you just let the hole get in the way is the simple key to improvement; if a golfer starts by putting towards cups and trying to make things, they will putt poorly for the rest of their life. This feels like a brand of 'Zen' but Jack is adamant about the effects of not perfecting this approach. He claims that anticipating results stays with a player forever. So he advises, rather than anticipating making or missing a putt, simply anticipate rolling or stroking the ball.

Jack argues that you can tell putting is in the mind just by watching people. He watches players making practice strokes and wonders what they're practising. Imagining himself doing the same thing, he realises that he wouldn't know which practice stroke to choose, which one he would actually try to use on the ball. This he regards as a pathetic waste of time. For Jack, the player who does this is just trying to do anything in order to avoid getting over the ball and stroking it.

Jackie was inducted into the World Golf Hall of Fame in 2000 as the first choice to be elected via the Veterans Category, which was formed to allow the World Golf Hall of Fame Advisory Board to consider players whose career occurred primarily before 1960. However, he is a man to keep his feet on the ground. He once said, 'I don't think what I did as a player is that important. I didn't think playing was a great achievement, because I always felt like I could play. I was playing a game.'

Jack remains an emotional man and has strong opinions about the modern game. He has said that golf is turning into something it wasn't meant to be, that a walking game has become a riding game. It annoys him that the sport has become expensive to play and regrets how the golf course has been transformed into 'a grassed-in office, a place for business instead of privacy and relaxation', and, in the last few years, Jack has sought to win golf back for the 'common man'. He feels that cutting ordinary people off from the game, alongside the rise of golf carts, which have caused caddies to disappear from the greens, has been detrimental to golf in America. Kids no longer grow up caddying and so are deprived of spending some time around adults and gradually growing into the game. Perhaps Jack's position is evidenced by the USA's continual failure in the Ryder Cup in the last six years.

Jack also has much to say about racism and golf. He was raised in a caddie yard, like most players were 50 or 60 years ago, and was one of only a few white boys there out of around 100 caddies. So, from his boyhood, he knew something of the problems that minority groups faced. In fact, he couldn't get into the clubhouse himself, in his own words: 'So I was raised pretty much "not being able to get in". Hell, even pros had trouble getting into the clubhouses back then! So I understand that completely.'

According to Jack, a large proportion of the discrimination that is experienced is based on economics. Corporations introduce mostly white people into country clubs, either directly, by making it part of a company benefit, or through the salaries they pay their employees that enable them to afford to become members of expensive clubs. This, of course, perpetuates extortionate membership costs; if people pay high membership fees, then the fees will remain high. But Jack believes that, if black people were in more prominent positions, golf clubs would have a more representative membership.

For Jack, a man who admits that he 'grew up shooting dice', golf is not for conservative people, as it is a risky game. Every shot has an element of jeopardy and Jack feels too many people try to play the game without taking chances. Once more, this might be seen as a dictum for life in a broader sense. A life without risk is a life half lived and much of our excitement in living arises from the chances we take rather than the constant quest for the illusion of safety.

Jack enjoyed his playing days. He fondly recalled how there would be dozens of players travelling around the country, often on the same road, on the way to the same competitions. It was not unusual for the golfers to pass one another during the night. Jack could recognise his colleagues and opponents, the likes of Jimmy Demaret and Johnny Revolta, by the cars they drove. It was like a convoy and they would meet up in a town on the road and eat. Jack loved driving through west Texas on a moonlit road.

Anyone meeting Jack for the first time might find him not a little daunting because of the sheer energy he exudes. Though well into his seventies, he acts like a man in his twenties.

A recipient of the PGA Tour Lifetime Achievement Award, Jack is a legend in golf and there is a consensus in the sport that he knows its intricacies and rules as well as anyone living. When asked about what made him a champion, he said that his business was the playing of the game and that the honing of judgement played a great part; the judgement of picking out a 5-iron over a 4-iron, the wind, the lines that he had. The minute Jack teed off he began to make judgements about the next shot, not waiting until he got to the ball.

But, more than anything else, Jack feels that it is his knowledge of the rules of golf that made him a great player. However, he sees a purpose in golf beyond the greens: 'Only in games do you learn rules … The only value games have is they keep civilisation reasonably civilised, because there are rules to conduct games.'

PGA TOUR WINS
1950 (4) Bing Crosby Pro-Am (tie with Dave Douglas, Smiley Quick, Sam Snead), Rio Grande Valley Open, St Petersburg Open, Sioux City Open
1952 (5) Texas Open, Houston Open, Baton Rouge Open, St Petersburg Open, Miami Open
1953 (1) Inverness Invitational
1956 (2) The Masters, PGA Championship
1958 (1) Insurance City Open Invitational
1959 (1) Houston Classic
1961 (1) Buick Open Invitational
1963 (1) Lucky International Open

CHAPTER FIVE

Let the Games Begin!

DAY ONE: 36-HOLE FOURSOMES

Jack Burke's faith in his team was high enough not to call on Lionel Hebert, the PGA Champion, during the first day. The confidence he had in the eight golfers he fielded was well repaid. The Americans all looked like hardened pros. The home team seemed, at first sight, to be a troop from an earlier era and carrying some of the baggage of a country yet to recover from war. The men from the USA came over as tough, while the Great Britain and Ireland side had more of a dour quality about them.

DOUG FORD AND DOW FINSTERWALD (USA)
V
PETER ALLISS AND BERNARD HUNT
(GREAT BRITAIN AND IRELAND)

The Friday-morning foursomes began in rather damp, overcast conditions. But it was quite warm, with a fresh breeze, as starter Hugh Docherty asked for 'Quiet, please'.

Finsterwald and Ford were the first US pairing. Ford was the reigning Masters Champion and the former (1955) US Open Champion. Ed Furgol once said of Ford, 'There are about 25 golfers on the Tour who can play as well as Doug, but Doug has the interest, enthusiasm and spirit they lack. He loves everything about the game of golf.'

Doug M Ford Sr was born on 6 August 1922 in West Haven, Connecticut, and grew up in New York City where his father was a driving-range pro. Doug was introduced to golf at the age of six, when his father's range was a convenient place to practise.

The young Ford was a fine third-baseman in semi-pro baseball and was offered a scholarship to Manhattan College. However, when he won the New York Junior Golf title, he decided to try to make it in that sport. He went on to win the Westchester County and New York Amateur Championships and toured the pro circuit for two years as an amateur, trying to decide whether his game was strong enough for him to make a living at it.

He turned professional in 1949 and won his first tournament, the Jacksonville Open, in 1952. His first Major victory was the 1955 PGA Championship. The tournament was still match-play when Doug defeated Cary Middlecoff in the final. Doug was that season's PGA Player of the Year, recording 20 top-10 finishes on the US Tour.

At this point, Doug had twice been the Tour's No. 2 money-winner, earning $26,815 in 1953 and $45,378 in 1957.

It was in 1957, starting the final round three strokes adrift of Sam Snead at the Augusta National (Ford is the holder of the record number of appearances in this event), that Doug scored a brilliant 66 (at that time the lowest final round ever recorded) to win the Masters by three from Snead, who did little wrong in his level-par round, to become one of only a handful of golfers to have captured the Open and the PGA Championship. That year, Doug was among the top-25 players in all the 32 events he played in. He was in the top 10 on 24 occasions and won three times.

The PGA Championship was won the year after Doug's victory by Dow H Finsterwald Sr. Finsterwald was born on 6 September 1929 in Athens, Ohio. His rise to becoming a tournament-winning golfer started with a dream fired by his passion for baseball; he didn't play the game, but kept box scores of Cincinnati Reds games, following information provided by broadcaster (and former ball player) Waite Hoyt on the radio. Dow wanted to go to a World Series. However, this required cash. It was 1945 and he was 15 when he took a summer job at the Athens Country Club. But, come the end of that summer, he didn't go to the World Series; he bought a set of golf clubs instead. In his own words, he was 'hooked and sliced'.

In 1957, Dow had perhaps the highest reputation among

the Americans at Lindrick, but is probably best known for winning the 1958 PGA Championship. Dow attended Ohio University in his home town. He led the institutional side, the 'Bobcats', to their first Mid-American Conference Golf title in 1951 by finishing runner-up to team-mate Dave Rambo in the 36-hole event.

Maybe remembering what had occurred in the latter part of the match at Wentworth in 1953, when Peter Alliss and Bernard Hunt had wavered in their critical single matches, Dai Rees put the two together to lead the home attack in the foursomes. By that time, both were leading tournament professionals in the UK. Rees understood that Hunt and Alliss wanted to atone for their surrenders of 1953.

Peter Alliss was born on Saturday, 28 February 1931 in Berlin, Germany. In all, he played 30 Ryder Cup matches in 1953, 1957, 1959, 1961, 1963, 1965, 1967 and 1969, winning 10, losing 15 and halving five.

The son of a professional golfer, Peter, who turned professional at the age of 15, looked to be the talented heir to Henry Cotton from the ranks of British post-war golfers. However, he never fulfilled that early promise. It has been suggested that from childhood the game came too easy to Alliss, and as such he did not develop the resolute attitude necessary to win a Major title. Although Peter inherited his father's beautifully straightforward and conventional style that, with his natural strength, meant he was able to hit the ball long and far, his father, Percy (born 1897), was a difficult act to follow. Allis Senior won 20 Major tournaments, including the British Match Play Championship in 1933 and 1937. Percy was also a member of four Ryder Cup sides and came third in the 1931 British Open and fourth another four times. Peter's best British Open placing was in joint eighth in 1954 and in 1969 he once more finished eighth.

Bernard Hunt came into this world in Atherstone (between Birmingham and Leicester), Warwickshire, England, on Sunday, 2 February 1930. His father was also a professional golfer and Bernard turned professional in 1946 at his parents' local club. Indeed, the Hunts were almost a golfing dynasty of sorts, and Bernard's brother, Geoff (five years his junior), would also play in the Ryder Cup in 1963.

Bernard won his first important professional event, the Sumrie, in 1953 and won it again exactly 20 years later. He became something of a legend in Britain over two decades and was one of the top players on the European circuit in the 1950s and 1960s. He led the Order of Merit (which was then points based) in 1958, 1960 and 1965.

Bernard won the Vardon Trophy (for the best stroke average throughout the season) on three occasions, in 1958, 1960 and 1965. This perhaps demonstrates his remarkable consistency and, although he was victorious in numerous important tournaments in the UK – the Bowmaker, Daks, Martini, the Dunlop Masters (twice), the Penfold and the Wills – he didn't threaten to win one of the Majors. But he did claim third place in the 1960 Open Championship at St Andrews and was fourth in 1964. He was also triumphant in the Belgian, German and French Opens.

Bernard possessed a short swing that he was able to replicate regularly, which Henry Cotton saw as 'one of the most precise and economical and brief actions of modern times'. Blessed with great composure, Bernard was also a fine putter.

In 1953, at Wentworth, Cotton was the non-playing captain of the Ryder Cup team in which Bernard made his debut. Regardless of his respect for Bernard's swing, Cotton counselled him to modify it, to make it longer and more upright. Bernard tried to follow the great man's guidance but the whole situation was not a pleasant memory for Bernard: 'It was Henry Cotton's fault. He told me that I would never be consistently good with that "awful" swing.'

Bernard's self-belief was further damaged when he viewed his swing for the first time on *Movietone News* at the cinema: 'I must confess it didn't look good. Until then I imagined it was just like Ben Hogan's. Anyway, I took Cotton's advice and tried to sort it out but struggled and eventually reverted to my old swing, which was short and flattish.'

Playing in Portugal years later, Bernard was asked to dinner by Cotton. Bernard reminded his host of the 'advice' he had given him, to which Cotton responded, 'I can't be right all the time.'

Over the next few days Bernard won the Algarve Open.

But, on that first morning of the 1957 Ryder Cup, perhaps nerves had an effect, and the Englishmen failed to even match par in the morning. The Americans shot straight threes at the first three holes and took a two-shot lead. Although finding themselves in the rough on half a dozen occasions over the first nine holes, the US pair made a series of fine resurgences, particularly so at the 7th, where a superb pitch by Finsterwald from the left-hand rough took the hole that had looked destined to be claimed by Hunt and Alliss. Out in 32 to 35, after nine holes, Finsterwald and Ford had a three-hole advantage over the Englishmen.

The Americans made par 4 at the 15th to pull four ahead, but they were hit hard when their opponents pulled back to be one down with one to play. But Hunt messed up a 50-inch putt on the 18th, so losing the opportunity to go into lunch level.

The start of afternoon play saw the Americans in even better form than they had demonstrated earlier. They took just a score of shots to play the first half-dozen holes. At the 8th (a 318-yarder), their three put them back to three ahead. But, regardless of the rash of low scoring, the US pair were unable to subdue their courageous rivals until the last but one hole, two and one.

HOLE BY HOLE – MATCH ONE																				
Players	1	2	3	4	5	6	7	8	9	Out	10	11	12	13	14	15	16	17	18	In
Ford & Finsterwald	3	3	3	4	4	3	4	4	4	32	3	4	3	4	5	4	5	4	4	36 68
Alliss & Hunt	4	4	3	4	4	3	5	4	4	35	3	3	4	5	4	3	4	4	4	34 69
Ford & Finsterwald	4	4	2	4	3	3	5	3	4	32	4	3	4	5	4	C	5	4		Won 2 & 1
Alliss & Hunt	4	4	3	4	4	3	4	4	4	34	4	3	4	5	5	W	4	4		

CHAPTER SIX

Making a Fight of It

ART WALL AND FRED HAWKINS (USA)
V
KEN BOUSFIELD AND DAI REES
(GREAT BRITAIN AND IRELAND)

Wall and Hawkins matched Ford and Finsterwald's 3 x 3 start, and also started their game at a hot pace, taking the first two holes with birdies.

Art Wall Jr, a six-foot-tall slim man, with the rhythmic swing, was born on 25 November 1923 in Honesdale, Pennsylvania. He began his pro career in 1949 after graduating from Duke University with a business degree. He was to make three appearances in the Ryder Cup in 1957, 1959 and 1961. He played six games in the competition, won four and lost two.

Art won his first tournament, the Fort Wayne Open, on 16 August 1953 and, although he only had two top 10s in the Masters, Wall was one of the game's most accurate players. An informal count reveals he recorded more than 40 aces during his career. However, it was a statistic he didn't much care for, which is why the count isn't official. He always felt people made too much of a commotion about such things.

Fred Hawkins was one of two golfing brothers (the other was Charles) from Antioch, Illinois. Fred played many years on the PGA Tour and what is now the Champions Tour.

Rees and the soft-spoken Bousfield held on to hit back by winning the 4th and 10th and then getting level on the last hole of the morning with a putt, just a foot short of five yards, by Rees.

The Americans nearly replicated their earlier form after lunch, snatching another two-shot lead at the 3rd and 4th. But the British duo came again and they were level by the 10th. But now they used the momentum to pressurise Hawkins and Wall and forced their opponents into making errors.

Although Bousfield was a member of the 1955 British Ryder Cup team at Thunderbird Ranch in California, illness had prevented him from playing. He was one of the leading British golfers of the immediate post-World War II period and was almost the archetypal English pro golfer of the 1950s. The son of a stationmaster, Bousfield was born on 2 October 1919. A member of six British Ryder Cup teams (1949, 1951, 1955, 1957, 1959 and 1961), he played 10 matches in all, winning half and losing half.

Ken became an assistant to Archie Compston at Coombe Hill at the age of 15, but it was not until after World War II, during which he had served in the Royal Marines, that Bousfield started to play in the bigger professional tournaments. His first notable win came during 1951 in the *News Chronicle* tournament. A couple of years earlier, in 1949, he had been selected to represent Great Britain in the Ryder Cup, when the Americans claimed a narrow two-point victory at Ganton. Bousfield won his only match in the foursomes in partnership with Fred Daly, against Bob Hamilton and Skip Alexander. The British pair sped to the turn in 33 shots and were two ahead at lunchtime. They won by four and two. Bousfield lined up once more for his country two years later at Pinehurst, but he and Daly were defeated by the daunting Ben Hogan and Jimmy Demaret.

Bousfield's most successful year in golf was 1955; he was all-conquering in the *News of the World* Match Play tournament, and he won the German Open and the inaugural British PGA Match Play Championship at Pannal. He met the distinguished match-player Eric Brown in the final of the tournament at Pannal and took the title with some excellent play. In the morning round, Bousfield scored 68, to put himself three holes up, but lost them all straight after lunch. But, demonstrating the cool determination that came to be associated with him, Bousfield came back to claim victory.

In the second game of the 1957 Ryder Cup, Bousfield made the winning putt on the 16th from 15 feet. Ken and Dai had clawed five holes back to win three and two.

The victory was a first in a foursomes match for Dai Rees in six Ryder Cup appearances. His previous best was a halved match in 1937, his first outing in the Cup. Three defeats had followed, and he had twice been obliged to take on no more than a spectator's role in foursomes matches.

Having levelled the overall match, Rees made his way out to the course to give his support in the remaining two foursomes.

Players	1	2	3	4	5	6	7	8	9	Out	10	11	12	13	14	15	16	17	18	In
HOLE BY HOLE – MATCH TWO																				
Wall & Hawkins	3	3	3	6	4	3	4	4	4	34	5	3	4	4	5	4	4	4	4	37 71
Bousfield & Rees	4	4	3	4	5	3	4	4	4	35	4	3	4	4	5	4	4	4	3	35 70
Wall & Hawkins	4	4	3	4	4	3	4	4	4	34	5	4	5	5	5	4	5			Won 3 & 2
Bousfield & Rees	4	4	4	5	4	3	4	3	4	35	4	3	5	4	5	4	4			

CHAPTER SEVEN

America Hit Back

TED KROLL AND JACK BURKE (USA)
V
MAX FAULKNER AND HARRY WEETMAN
(GREAT BRITAIN AND IRELAND)

Of all the four foursomes matches, this encounter had the least quality. Kroll and Burke were forced to fight all the way against Weetman and Faulkner, who at no point looked likely to stop working.

In 2004, Bernard Hunt said that Ted Kroll was similar to Mark O'Meara in that he had a shortish swing, but he rifled it. To Bernard, Ted seemed so relaxed and his swing was fantastic; and Bernard liked him as a man, perhaps above all other American players he had known.

Ted J Kroll was born on 4 August 1919 in New Hartford, New York, and was selected for the Ryder Cup in 1953, 1955 and 1957. He played four games, winning three and losing one.

Lucky to be able to play golf at all, Ted was wounded on four occasions during World War II, serving as a sergeant in the US Army. He earned three Purple Hearts.

Having begun his 34-year PGA Tour career in 1949, Ted won eight times on the Tour, including three wins in 1956, when he topped the money list with earnings of $72,836.

Ted's best finishes in Major tournaments were a second place in the US PGA Championship in 1956, losing in the final to Jack Burke Jr, three and two, and sharing the runner-up spot in the 1960 US Open.

In the Ryder Cup, Ted was a highly successful foursomes player, winning all his matches – twice alongside Jack Burke and once with Doug Ford. However, he was well beaten by Fred Daly in their 1953 singles match at Wentworth. Chick Harbert, his captain in the match two years later, clearly remembered this defeat, as he did not ask Ted to take part in the singles that year. But, by 1957, it seems that Ted was exonerated and he was due to meet Peter Mills, before being obliged to withdraw through illness.

For several years, Ted's score of 60 in the 1954 Texas Open was a record for 18 holes.

In his later years, he built a reputation as a sort of 'golf doctor', an individual to whom other professionals looked for analysis of their problems with their swing and/or stance.

At Lindrick, the third US pairing had a one-hole advantage after the first nine holes but could not improve on that by lunch. However, during the afternoon, by the turn, the Americans had gained a four-hole lead, having got to that point in 33 strokes. Out of the blue, Weetman seemed to find the fairways overly narrow.

In his era, Harry Weetman was one of the most sparkling players to watch. He was sometimes able to make unbelievable recoveries from almost impossible spots in the heavy rough.

Harry was from the West Midlands, born in Oswestry, Shropshire, on 25 October 1920, and he appeared in the Ryder Cup in 1951, 1953, 1957, 1959, 1961, 1963 and captained the Great Britain and Ireland team in 1965.

Looking at Harry's build, you might have guessed he was a county-level fast bowler, or a goalkeeper from the lower leagues of professional football. He was a big man, with broad shoulders, and his game was set on his enormous legs. He had hands like shovels on the end of long muscular arms. As such, he had the capability to fire a golf ball a huge distance; when on his game, he was one of the finest pitchers in Britain. The enormous strength of his forearms, wrists, hands and fingers enabled Harry, at points, to rescue himself in spectacular fashion and draw gasps of disbelief from the gallery. With this great reservoir of force from the elbows down, he could retain his grip through almost any adversity without becoming tensed up; hence, he kept the club head swinging through the thick of the most desperate fights.

Harry became a golf professional quite by chance. Unlike many players of his era (for instance, the Whitcombes, the Bradbeers, the Cawseys and the Trapps), Harry did not come from a golfing dynasty, and was the first of his family to take up the game. He might not have done so at all if the garden of his childhood home had not looked out on to the local golf course, Aston Park.

As a boy, Harry watched the golfers and, like many others before him, made his first club out of a piece of wood. Seeing how enthusiastic the young Weetman lad was, the local professional, James Walker (who was to hold sway at the Shrewsbury Club), gave him a job in his shop. When Harry reached 15, Jim took him on as his assistant. Harry was always conscious of his debt to Walker.

About a year later, Harry became assistant to WB Fenton at the Leek Club, Staffordshire, and after another year took up a similar role with JW Musty at Borth, in Cardiganshire. This was his first experience of real links, and playing under seaside conditions helped Harry improve his game enormously.

At the age of 18, in 1938, Harry entered the Welsh Professional Championship, held at Royal St David's, Harlech. He was already hitting the ball a long way and he overheard Ken Williams, the well-known Welsh professional, saying, 'If I could hit the ball like that, I would go round in 59!'

Harry was nearly 19 in 1939 when World War II broke out. While making up his mind what to do, he was offered the job of golf coach to Bromsgrove School, a renowned public school in the Midlands that had moved from close to Birmingham to Llanwrtyd Wells because of the threat of bombing. There, Harry taught the game to 250 boys, thus anticipating by more than a decade the Golf Foundation scheme under which the sport would be taught to schoolchildren all over Britain.

When he turned 20, Harry joined the RAF as an armourer. After a couple of years, when there was a call for volunteers for Army armoured units, he transferred to the First Battalion of the Welsh Regiment, and was attached to the famous Sixth Armoured Division.

It was not until he was in Italy in 1944 that Harry's thoughts began to turn again towards golf. He had a heavy weighted club sent out from the UK and he deployed it regularly in an attempt to get his swing moving smoothly again. At the end of the War, he brought the club back to the UK and it remained in his possession for the rest of his life.

Before he was demobbed from the Army, Harry played in the Victory Golf tournament at St Andrews, but he failed to score well. Golf naturally seemed strange after five years in the service of King and country, but Harry managed to attune his muscles again by doing some tree-felling.

Harry's first post-war job was as assistant to WR Firkins at Stourbridge. He was offered a job in Switzerland, but turned it down, and moved to the London area to assist Pat Keene at the Hartsbourne Country Club, Bushey. The club was to prove a fine school for young assistants, including Eric Brown, Tony Fisher, Tony Harmon and Bernard and Geoffrey Hunt who went there with their father. Harry learned a lot in Bushey, including the change from the old-fashioned two-handled grip to the more 'natural' overlapping or 'Vardon' grip.

In 1947, while at Hartsbourne, Harry entered his first Open Championship. This was the year that Fred Daly won at Hoylake. Although he played reasonably well, Harry did not qualify for the last day's play. He didn't enter the 1948 event at Muirfield, but played regularly every year from 1949. Harry won the PGA Assistants' Championship in 1949 and 1950. Along with Dai Rees (1935 and 1936), Harry was the only player to win two Assistants' Championship back to back. Indeed, there is only one other golfer, Matthew Tottey, who has won that title twice.

Harry played 15 games in the Ryder Cup; he lost 11 times, had two victories and halved twice. It is puzzling why his record in the competition was so mediocre, because his style suited match-play, as evidenced by his fine performances in the PGA Match Play Championship, what was probably the most difficult professional event at the time. From 1951 to 1960, Harry won the title twice and got to the final five times. His first big success came in 1951 at Hoylake where he beat Jack Hargreaves, and then, on the same day, he defeated Flory van Donck and the phenomenal Henry Cotton, an amazing achievement. He was two holes down to Cotton but, in an exciting fightback, emblematic of Harry's play, he covered 12 holes in seven under fours.

Ruggedly strong, Harry's game through the green was premised on power and aggression. Cotton noted that Harry stayed behind the ball and hit past his body against a braced left side. In competition, he had a pugnacious attitude, seeming to be intent on smashing the ball to pieces, lashing into long shots with a frightening ferocity. Harry may have been erratic with the woods but his belligerence was tempered by a dexterous touch around the greens and his putting was a match for anyone in Europe. He was a maestro with a remarkable 'feel' for a shot when it came to pitching and putting, having the ability to consistently lay the ball close from a bunker. With a routine that was marked by a 'no frills' character, Harry's putts were carried out with a relaxed clean stroke.

Harry's entertaining play could captivate the watcher, and, although his meteor-like drives could land him in trouble, his ability to recover was unrivalled. However, by hitting the ball so hard, Harry sometimes strained too much and this meant he could be fallible off the tee. If, like Sam Snead and Jack Nicklaus, he had learned to control all that force, he almost certainly would have gained even more success.

For all this, Harry was amongst Britain's top golfers throughout the 1950s and early 1960s. As well as his Match Play Championship record, in 1952, Harry won the Dunlop Masters, a tournament restricted to the best golfers of the season, at the Mere Club, Cheshire, the first of his two victories in this event. He also won the German Open and the Swallow-Penfold on four occasions. He was awarded the Vardon Trophy in 1952 and 1958 and represented England in the Canada Cup four times.

This said, Harry was unable to make a mark in the Open Championship: he finished equal fifth at St Andrews in 1955 and his best placing was at Portrush in 1951 when he finished joint fourth.

As Match Play Champion, Harry was an automatic choice for the Ryder Cup in 1951, at Pinehurst, but in the singles he was trounced by the sturdy Lloyd Mangrum. Two years later, in the very close match at Wentworth, Harry and Peter Alliss probably should have scraped a half in their foursomes against Dave Douglas and Ed Oliver, but it was mistakes by Harry on the 35th hole that resulted in their eventual defeat.

But Harry exonerated himself against Sam Snead. By lunch, Snead was four holes ahead and, with six holes to play, nothing had changed. However, errors from the American, together with Harry's magnificent golf, resulted in the Brit winning five holes in succession. He held Snead off down the final hole for a marvellous win.

In 1955, at the Thunderbird Club, the match went to the USA and Harry was defeated in both his matches.

On 30 January 1956, Harry recorded the lowest score (58) on a long course in the UK on the 6,170-yard Croham Hurst Course in Croydon, Surrey.

But, at Lindrick in 1957, Harry was unable to achieve any consistency of strike and, by the 15th, with his partner faring no better, he was defeated; the British duo were easily beaten four and three.

HOLE BY HOLE – MATCH THREE																				
Players	1	2	3	4	5	6	7	8	9	Out	10	11	12	13	14	15	16	17	18	In
Kroll & Burke	3	4	4	5	4	3	4	4	4	35	4	4	4	4	5	3	5	4	3	36 71
Faulkner & Weetman	4	4	3	4	5	3	4	5	4	36	4	3	4	5	4	3	5	4	3	36 72
Kroll & Burke	4	4	2	5	4	3	4	3	4	33	5	3	5	4	4	4				Won 4 & 3
Faulkner & Weetman	5	4	3	5	4	3	4	4	4	36	5	4	4	4	4	4				

CHAPTER EIGHT

Struck by 'Thunder' Bolt

DICK MAYER AND TOMMY BOLT (USA)
V
CHRISTY O'CONNOR AND ERIC BROWN (GREAT BRITAIN
AND IRELAND)

Alvin Richard 'Dick' Mayer, born on 28 August 1924 in Stamford, Connecticut, was the US Open Champion of 1957 (won at Inverness, Florida). His appearances in the Ryder Cup of 1957 were to be his first and last.

Mayer nearly won the 1954 US Open, but a triple-bogey on the final hole left him tied for third, two shots back. He and Tommy Bolt (who would take Mayer's title from him in 1958) made a formidable pairing and were definitely the USA's strongest team.

It is a pity that the huge store of fables focusing on 'Thunder' Bolt's legendary bad temper has obscured his considerable reputation as a golfer. He had a superb golf swing, which was one of the most respected during his era, but also great elegance and invention that together made him one of best shot-makers of his time. Lee Trevino rated him amongst the most imaginative of all golfers. Although he wasn't the best putter in the world, the quality of other aspects of his game made up for that deficit. But Bolt's fallibility on the greens was alarmingly frustrating for a man of uneven disposition. However, he is recognised as one of the great characters of post-war golf.

Tommy Bolt has been a voice of reality in pro golf, the modern incarnation of which he has called 'dull' and being 'a chorus line of blond towheads you can't even tell apart'. He has had the epithets of 'Terrible', 'Tempestuous', 'Thunder' and 'Terrible-Tempered' attached to his name, but he was born Thomas Henry Bolt on 31 March 1918 in Haworth, Oklahoma. Soon after, he crossed the Red River in a covered wagon, moving to Paris, Texas. Ninety years later, he still has the knuckles of a carpenter and the bearing of a drill sergeant. He's in good enough physical shape not to look out of place in natty golf gear and he still has the face reminiscent of a cross between an ancient Irish bare-fist boxer and an antediluvian Native American warrior.

Before World War II when Tommy began his career, golf was often more dramatic in a physical sense. One American player had the habit of beating his right hand against the nearest tree trunk whenever it let him down. Another character, following a poor round, adopted the custom of going through his bag and smashing his clubs one by one. On one occasion, the set he became intent on destroying had been loaned. The distraught owner could merely stand by protesting. Many players have been known to storm off the course, or fail to start, when temper got the better of them, but Bolt was the first to make a regular performance out of golfing truculence.

Tommy's interest in golf began when he and his brother started caddying at Lakeside Golf Course in Shreveport, Louisiana. Tom caddied for pros like Al Espinosa, who lost the 36-hole US Open play-off at Winged Foot in 1929 to Bobby Jones, and Espinosa was to play a part in setting Tommy on his life path. When Tommy was 13, Espinosa arrived at Shreveport Country Club wearing wingtip golf shoes and carrying the biggest golf bag Tommy had ever seen before or since. Espinosa carried 30 clubs, and Tommy caddying for him must have resembled that scene in *Caddyshack* where the little kid tries to carry Rodney Dangerfield's bag. Tommy could barely lift the huge burden. But the way Espinosa dressed and carried himself, and those wingtip shoes, made the young Bolt think he was the biggest man in the world. That was when Tommy decided he wanted to be a golf player.

The Great Depression was just beginning to bite, Al Capone was in jail and Hollywood had not long started making talking pictures. Prohibition was still in effect and the stock market crashed. Charles Lindbergh had flown to Paris; Lou Gehrig was catching Babe Ruth; Jack Dempsey and Gene Tunney were stars of the ring; and Bobby Jones ruled the fairways.

At this time, Tommy was selling newspapers on a street corner. The first thing he did when he opened his bundle was go to the comic strips and read 'Ben Webster – Bound to Win'. Ben Webster was a little kid who was always overcoming obstacles to win things, marble-shooting contests and so on.

Like young Tommy, Ben was a poor boy and so the comic character became something of role model for Tommy. In 1958, on his way to winning the US Open, on a fateful Saturday at Southern Hills, he said to himself, 'Bound to Win ... Ben Webster ... Bound to Win.' It made him feel like he had a little extra something behind him.

As a boy, Tommy never had shoes that fitted him. On the first date he ever had, he borrowed a pair of his older brother's shoes. They were a size 9½, but Tommy was a size 10, and they hurt his feet so badly that he forgot to kiss the girl goodnight. Later on, he played in tournaments wearing shoes he'd borrowed. As shoes had always been a problem, when he could finally afford them, he went overboard and, at one point, Tommy owned *70* pairs of shoes. Even now, he can't help but take good care of them. He walks around in them like a cat for fear of wearing them out. He has a pair that are more than 30 years old, but they look new.

By his early twenties, Tommy had become a more than capable player, but he didn't have any money to prove it. He had to work, as a carpenter, and of course there was the Army.

Before he turned pro, Tommy made a living playing the amateur circuit around Shreveport. As the best player in town, he was able to sell the first-place merchandise prize before the tournament even started. He would already have the cash spent before he teed off, which meant he would have to win to avoid getting in big trouble with whoever had bought the prize. He recalled, 'That was pressure, boy. But most of the time Old Dad [as he calls himself] came through.'

For a long time, Tommy had an endorsement contract with

a Scotch-whisky importer. The company reimbursed him for what he drank, and paid him extra besides. Tommy found it hard to 'stay off the sauce' when he was as good as paid to drink it. Fortunately, he didn't become an alcoholic, but at one point he admitted he was drinking more than was good for him. It was his dermatologist, of all people, who convinced him to ease off. He went to see him about his nose, which had become big and red, and was told that it was because of the Scotch. For years after that, Tommy used his nose as an alcohol barometer.

Although Tommy would become infamous for his temper, he insisted that his own rages were nothing compared to that of JB, his older brother. When the siblings were teenagers, they pooled their money and bought a set of hickory-shafted irons. One day JB had a bad hole, and Tommy watched his brother go to the side of the green and shatter every one of the clubs against a tree. It made Tommy cry, but he was afraid to say anything to JB for fear he might turn his anger on him rather than the clubs.

Tommy spent four years and part of World War II in the US Army, and while stationed in Italy he became the head golf pro at one of Rome's elite golf clubs. This gave him a chance to continue to work on his game. The course only had 16 holes because Mussolini, who was not in favour of Italians watching golf, had shut down the two holes that weren't concealed by trees. Soldiers on furlough would come to the course, and, to give them something extra to do, Tommy built a big craps table and ran a dice game. He left Italy with a footlocker crammed full of cash, something close to $50,000 in lira. On the troop ship home, Tom fell in with what he called 'a bunch of criminals – American soldiers who had spent most of their hitch in the brig'. He started another dice game, but this group were streetwise and knew how to roll dice. Within three days, Tom had lost all his wartime winnings. By the time he hit port, his gambling habit was cured forever.

Some people might have jumped overboard. But money never meant much to Bolt, and he knew he could still make a living as a golf pro or, at the very least, go back to being a carpenter. He just shrugged it off and moved on: Ben Webster – Bound to Win.

After the War, Tommy bounced back and forth between competing on the Tour and retreating to construction work (in all, he spent 10 years in the industry) when he ran out of money. He had to ride the buses, stay at YMCAs, eat at the cafeterias, shooting 65s in the final rounds and winning $170. But, for all the discomfort, this was a time Tommy remembers fondly.

At Lindrick in the final foursomes of the 1957 Ryder Cup, O'Connor and Brown were the first Great Britain and Ireland couple to take the lead. That was at the 3rd, where Bolt missed a putt of little more than 18 inches. But O'Connor had a bad drive at the 4th, and Brown was equally remiss at the 7th; this left Mayer and Bolt one up. The Americans shot the outward half in 33, yet they were still only one up, with Brown and O'Connor making amends for their undistinguished driving with stroke-saving pitching and putting. (It wasn't until the 10th hole of the morning that either of the home pairing placed a tee-shot on the fairway.)

The Great Britain and Ireland pair were still only one down

after 14 holes. Bolt put his approach in a bunker at the 14th, but O'Connor failed with a very short putt at the 15th and Brown hooked his approach at the 16th, so both holes went to the USA side. Mayer and Bolt retained that three-hole lead at the end of the first round, for which their score was 67, the best performance of any pair in the morning's play. Brown and O'Connor had scored 71.

But, in spite of the remarkable figures attained by the American duo, they were just three to the good, O'Connor and Brown having done well to weather the Yankee storm.

Christy O'Connor said of his Ryder Cup record that it was 'not a very good one because as one of the leading team members I was required to play in more matches with limited rest periods'.

He scored 11 wins and four halves from 36 games.

At Royal County Down in 1954, Harry Bradshaw defeated a professional from Bundoran in a 36-hole play-off for the Irish Professional Championship. After the match, 'The Brad' said, 'I'm afraid I'm on the way out … This young man, Christy O'Connor, is the player to watch out for in the future.'

Patrick Christopher O'Connor was born in County Galway at Knocknagarra, near Salthill, not far from the city of Galway, on 21 December 1924. He grew up on his family's farm that bordered the 1st green at Galway Golf Club. Watching the play captivated the youngster but his father could never understand his son's fascination with a game, insisting it 'was going to get him nowhere'.

But, as soon as Christy was able to get over the boundary

wall, he knew he had found his vocation. He was to appear in every Ryder Cup from 1955 to 1973 (10 in all, which gave him a place in *Guinness Book of Records*, a record only broken by Nick Faldo in 1997).

Christy learned his golf via caddying and green-keeping, taking up the assistant's role under then club professional Bob Wallace. He recalled, 'I wanted to be a player. In those early days, I learned a lot from Bob Wallace … I loved playing and I worked very hard to be a good player. You don't get it just by thinking about it.'

Christy's ability was evident to those who saw him play as a young man at Galway and later at Tuam, where he moved to in 1948, taking on a sort of dual role of green-keeper and professional. There was overall agreement that he was a golfer who would be able to compete with the finest. But his early progress was blocked by the Irish Professional Golfers Association. In 1948, he was refused entry to the Irish Championship staged at the Galway club and it took him half a decade to get membership of the association (he was finally accepted in 1951) and become eligible to play in official events. By that time, he had developed a strong sense of antipathy and irritation at the unfairness of a structure that had stopped him from competing against men of his own calibre.

This being the case, when Christy finally started to compete in earnest, a dangerous competitor had been let loose. His drive and determination were palpable as he stepped on to any course.

Although Christy's match-play record is not exceptional,

with him winning the British Match Play Championship just once, Christy is amongst the finest golfers produced by Ireland. He was the first professional golfer from the British Isles to win four-figure prize money, and, in the 1970 John Player Classic at Hollinwell in Nottinghamshire, the first to win a five-figure cheque (pounds sterling). This meant he won more than twice as much money as anyone else on the British circuit that year. By that time, his victory total was over 20. From the mid-1950s, he was one of the leading money-winners in professional golf; between 1955 and 1970, he was never lower than 10th in the money list and was second seven times.

One of the first to note Christy's potential was Eric Brown. The hardy Scotsman, who would be amongst Christy's toughest opponents on the European circuit, but also one of his best friends. Before the young man from Knocknagarra had even hit a shot in his first British Open Championship at Royal Portrush, Brown said, 'There is an Irish lad here who reminds me of Sam Snead; his swing is a gift from God and he rips the ball a country mile.'

Following a 19th-place finish in the 1951 British Open in Royal Portrush, which was won by Max Faulkner, who took home the £300 in prize money – which seems paltry, by today's standards – Christy moved from Galway to become the professional at Bundoran Golf Club in Donegal, where he would serve from 1951 to 1957.

Christy made his first significant mark on Irish golf in 1953 by winning the Ulster Championship and the Irish Dunlop title. In 1955, he won his second Irish Dunlop crown and was a top-10 finisher in the Open Championship at St Andrews, which got him a place on the Ryder Cup team.

In the last foursomes of the 1957 Ryder Cup, the Celtic couple managed to compensate for a number of unforced errors to keep their adversaries in striking distance. Brown's best drive of the match helped the pair make a winning birdie three at the first hole in the afternoon. But their luck deserted them. The Americans won the 21st and 22nd and thereafter didn't make one mistake. They played the initial nine holes after lunch one shot better than they had in the morning, putting themselves six holes ahead and went to the turn in the afternoon round in 32 strokes. The US twosome made birdies at the par-4 12th and par-5 13th, and were suitably rewarded with a seven and five victory.

Although O'Connor and Brown had played par-golf throughout the game, they had been effectively demolished by the focused and talented Americans. Mayer's play with Bolt had been brilliant.

But the defeat seemed to make O'Connor and Brown more determined to make a mark before the match was out. Eric Brown was certainly not a man to accept defeat lightly. He came seemingly from nowhere to win the Scottish Amateur Championship, a match-play event, in 1946 and turned professional the same year. Held back by the rule that dictated that a professional needed to wait for five years before entering a major PGA tournament, he was limited to local and European events. But when his time was up he was a powerful presence on the British tournament circuit and in 1957 won the Dunlop Masters.

Brown won the Scottish Professional Championship seven times between 1956 and 1968 and represented his country in the Canada Cup every year from 1954 to 1962 and in 1966 and 1967.

Brown finished third in the Open of 1957 and, in 1958, when he got to the last hole at Royal Lytham, he knew that a par would probably win it for him. After driving into a bunker, he took half-a-dozen and missed the play-off by a shot that in the end pitted Peter Thomson against Dave Thomas. So Brown's 279, including a brilliant third-round 65, was only good enough to once more give him third place.

Even after the hiding Mayer and Bolt gave O'Connor and Brown, and despite the fact that they were down 3–1, Eric Brown still felt the Americans could be defeated. For him, it had been a quality match (the number of American under-pars and threes went into double figures) and he had no doubts that Mayer and Bolt had played supremely well in the foursomes, but he was to admit that the wayward long game played by both Christy and himself had helped their opponents no end.

For the third time Brown was in a losing couple in the Ryder Cup and was to comment, 'I had had a bellyful of it in Ryder Cup foursomes.' He noted that Bolt was 'most jovial' in the foursomes and Brown saw good reason for this as his partner especially showed the home pair how devastating American putting can be. But Brown was to break Bolt's buoyant mood long before the last ball of the 1957 Ryder Cup was sunk.

HOLE BY HOLE – MATCH FOUR

Players	1	2	3	4	5	6	7	8	9	Out	10	11	12	13	14	15	16	17	18	In
Mayer & Bolt	4	4	4	4	3	3	3	4	4	33	4	3	3	4	5	4	4	4	3	34 67
O'Connor & Brown	4	4	3	5	3	3	5	4	4	35	4	4	3	4	4	5	5	4	3	36 71
Mayer & Bolt	4	4	2	3	4	3	4	4	4	32	5	3	3	3						Won 7 & 5
O'Connor & Brown	3	4	3	4	4	4	5	4	4	35	4	3	3	5						

CHAPTER NINE

Mighty Max

After the first day of the 1957 Ryder Cup, the USA led Great Britain and Ireland 3–1. It seemed that a familiar story of American supremacy was unfolding and that disaster loomed. But Dai Rees was not disheartened. He went to each member of his team, and told them that they personally had an outstanding chance of winning.

Wanting to make a fight of it in the singles the next day, the Great Britain and Ireland captain got his players together and talked about team selection. He also called for the day's scorecards to analyse what had gone wrong and who had played poorly. But he knew Faulkner and Weetman had trouble breaking 80 in the morning and had been even less impressive during the afternoon. Demanding an open debate, Faulkner instantly admitted to playing 'rubbish' and requested not to be considered for the singles.

Herbert Gustavus Max Faulkner was born on Saturday, 29 July 1916 in Bexhill, East Sussex. He played in the Ryder Cups of 1947, 1949, 1951, 1953 and 1957. Always better adapted to match-play than stroke-play, he gained just a single win and seven losses. But this record does not reflect his great contribution to the teams he played in. Faulkner won almost every major British championship.

Max was the first child of Gustavus Faulkner, who was the professional at the Bexhill club in 1919 and had once served as assistant to James Braid at Walton. Max said of his father's prowess in terms of striking the ball, 'He couldn't half hit it.'

Max's two brothers would also become golf professionals.

Faulkner Senior won the *Western Mail* tournament, was runner-up in the Welsh Open and had come close to selection for the Ryder Cup team in 1931. He became the professional at Pennard, on the Gower Peninsula, so Max started his education in South Wales. He recalled, 'I lived there until I was 10 which is why I have a slight Welsh lilt in my voice. I began my golf there at four-and-a-half and in 1926 we moved to Bramley.'

Max's all-round sporting skill was quickly recognised; he showed a particular talent for football. But predictably golf was his main interest. The Faulkner family moved to the club at Bramley, south of Guildford, where, at 14, Max started to work as his father's assistant and played to two. Gus supported his son's ambitions in the game and the boy learned well. He began to build the foundations of the splendid full and free-flowing Faulkner swing that would inspire so many imitators.

It was at Bramley, at the age of 15, that Max won a junior

tournament by 15 strokes, with a round of 68. Following that, his career path seemed obvious. It was around this time that Gus, ignoring the rules, managed to enter his son for the Open at Sandwich. The teenager's play was decent enough, but he failed to make the cut.

After turning professional in 1933, Max left home and got his first assistant's job at Sonning Golf Club in Reading, Berkshire. By the late 1930s, Max Faulkner was the professional at Leamington Spa and began to make his mark in tournaments.

The years just before World War II looked promising for Max. In 1938, he married Joan Weller and, in 1939, led the Open at St Andrews after the first round. Looking back, Max reflected, 'My four great pals were Jimmy Adams, Dai Rees, Ken Bousfield and Harry Weetman. I was making my way then and very fit.'

However, the young Faulkner's career was interrupted by the War. In 2001, he reflected on the damage that this had probably done to his career. He only played one round of golf between 1939 and 1945 when he was in the RAF. If the conflict had not interrupted his career, Max believed that he might have won the Open three or four times.

According to Max, he personally had a 'lucky war', although, tragically, Max's younger brother Frank was killed at Dunkirk the day his commission came through.

During the years of hostility, Max was a Physical Training Instructor with the RAF. He played very little golf during wartime, but he recalled one of those rare occasions: 'Henry Cotton was an admin officer in the RAF and he knew I was at

Whitley Bay. He asked me to play in a Red Cross match and, when we met, I saluted him. He said, "Cut that out", and had my clubs sent up.'

However, in the RAF, Max took up boxing and became a services champion, fighting at middleweight. He lost just one fight and that was to an old pro.

After his time in the forces, Max began playing in tournaments with a mixture of enjoyment and adventure in a style unique to himself. On one occasion, saying he needed to get the blood to his brain, he walked from a green to the next tee on his hands!

In 1945, Max instantly demonstrated that he had lost none of his golfing ability, finishing runner-up in the Victory tournament at St Andrews. He remembered, 'There were lots of players in those days that, at the start of a tournament, had a good chance of winning. Nowadays you can count the likely winners on one hand.'

For a brief period, Max served as assistant to Henry Cotton at the Royal Mid-Surrey. However, he wanted his independence, and, in 1948, acting on his father's idea, his family clubbed together to buy the course at Selsey, near Chichester, for him. Gus believed this would give his son the time and space to practise without hindrance, telling Max, 'I'll buy Selsey and you'll win the Open.'

The heaving of prawn pots every day off Selsey Bill, together with years of making and repairing clubs, helped Max develop powerful hands and forearms. And perhaps it was the work professionals did on clubs that gave that generation of players such extraordinarily strong hands.

In 1947, Max was selected for the Ryder Cup in Portland, Oregon. After disembarking from the *Queen Mary*, the British and Irish players faced a train journey of several days and Max provided knowledgeable observations about landmarks passed during the trip.

Max had a Ryder Cup debut of fire. Alongside Jimmy Adams, he faced Ben Hogan and Jimmy Demaret, two pillars of the US team. But the British pair refused to be intimidated and were four up at the turn and still two in front at lunch. With the match level, the 34th hole was a decisive point. The Americans were bunkered off the tee, but they made a birdie, and went on to win the match by two holes.

In the singles, Max faced Lloyd Mangrum, another great player. Max marched on to the course in a positive mood but once more tasted defeat.

Max remembered the team being called to Cotton's hotel room before a ball was hit and being asked to kneel down as the captain read a prayer. It seems that plea for divine intervention was not heard. The 11–1 score line turned out to be the heaviest defeat ever inflicted by the Americans in the Ryder Cup.

Two years later, at Ganton, Faulkner and Adams were out first against 'Dutch' Harrison and Johnny Palmer. All day, the British played superbly and won on the 35th hole. However, Harrison's retribution in the singles was fierce. Dutch made five threes in his initial half-dozen holes, to go four up; he was seven up at lunch after a round of 67. Max was unable to make an impression against such fine play and was beaten, as was his team, seven points to five.

Max Faulkner was an uncommon man; a mercurial personality, he was amongst the most compelling characters in the history of golf and had an innate aptitude for many sports. He was an imposing, strong man, just under six foot tall, and he remained tremendously fit throughout his playing days, with a magnificent physique that, even in later years, put younger men to shame. The most striking parts of Faulkner's game were his woods and long irons. Although he habituated a stooped posture that gave his swing a rather awkward look, he had splendid rhythm and a very wide arc to his natural and uninhibited swing. He once said, 'The best swinger I ever saw was Richard Burton who won the Open in 1939.'

But, for all this, he never really modelled himself on anyone. When it came to striking the ball, Max combined power and control in such a way that he was a match for anyone in the sport. He said that his favourite golf shot was the drive with a following wind. Certainly, from a fan's perspective, there were few more stirring moments than when 'Mighty Max', feet anchored wide, swung with all his easy authoritative strength. In fact, it might have been too simple for him, as often he would experiment to provide himself a novel challenge.

At the peak of his powers, Max won numerous long-driving contests against the likes of Harry Weetman. As a putter, he had a very true, subtle touch and he gained some notoriety for his use of some peculiar homemade putters; the more eccentric their shape the more likely they were to please him. It was not unusual to find him playing with irons with different heads and shafts, and, in fact, he was a skilled maker of golf clubs. He had a great feel for the shape and flight of shots and a 'portfolio' of trick shots. He was one of the small number of players of his era with the ability to bend lofted approaches into the green, an amazing achievement with the relatively unsophisticated clubs of the time. It has even been said that Max was the first golfer to shape lofted approaches to the green.

Max hardly ever limited himself to the conventional set of 14 clubs and was endlessly looking to find a putter that would suit him perfectly (it is believed he had over 300). This perhaps demonstrated an ongoing problem with this aspect of his game. During the Dunlop Masters in 1960, in which he tied for runner-up spot, Max deployed a putter with a homemade head fastened to an ancient hickory shaft. This was characteristic of his energetic zeal when it came to perfecting his golf and innovating within the game. But he had an instinctive capability when it came to golf and his experimentation was as much to do with his fascination for the sport as anything else.

Invariably well turned out, Max was the first British professional to don bright apparel. He was sometimes called the 'Clown Prince of Golf' and, in dowdy, grey, post-war Britain, kept sober by clothing coupons and 'utility' goods, Max was like a rainbow in an overcast sky with his ostentatiously vivid but co-ordinated attire. For example, in the final round of the 1951 Open, he strode out in a shirt with blue and white stripes, canary-yellow plus-twos with matching socks and handmade shoes! Although, for some, at times, his colour schemes were a little too flamboyant, he had a touch of the harlequin in his style, with one rather more sombre commentator suggesting that he might have found fame in the music hall if he had not been such a gifted golfer.

It seems the motivation for adopting his colourful persona came from a spell in hospital during the War when he was suffering from a perforated ear drum. Each morning the nurses brought beautiful flowers into the ward, and every evening they took them out. Without those flowers, the ward seemed colourless and Max thought, if he got out of the War a fit man, he was going to make sure his dress was colourful.

But the Tsars of the clubhouses were not best pleased with such 'exhibitionism' during an era when professionals were expected to 'know their place'. When Max arrived early at Sandwich to practise for the Open of 1949, he was banned from the changing rooms and told to dress in the workshop.

In common with most professionals, with the exception of public-school-educated Henry Cotton, Max was required to operate within the unyielding class structure of the time. He remembered a typical rebuff by the celebrated golf writer Bernard Darwin when Max came into what Darwin saw as too close proximity: 'Don't you realise, Faulkner, that I am talking to a gentleman?'

Max's closeness to the two 'nobs' was unintended but crotchety Darwin took his opportunity to put a professional in his place.

For all his light-hearted gregariousness, Max had to deal with the strains of competing as much as anyone else. But his presence on golf courses was a great boost for players and fans and his example lead the way to a revival in brighter dress that was powerfully encouraged by the coming of colour television. Max was a likeable, jolly and personable man, who would engage with anyone within talking distance. A poor shot or a dreadful round did not elicit a frown or melodramatics, but was more likely to produce an excuse, a funny remark and an expectation that better things were to come.

Max seemed to relish big events. In the 1949 British Open, he was one stroke behind the leader at one stage. In his 86th year, Max reflected that he'd been close to winning that tournament. He was in the lead after three rounds at Sandwich that year, but faded to sixth. He was fifth at Troon the following year. Both times Max finished four strokes behind the winner, Bobby Locke, of South Africa.

However, in July 1951 at Royal Portrush, County Antrim, Max's putting was consistently good and, on the superb and extremely fast greens, he was particularly accurate.

Jimmy Adams was the first-round leader after a dramatic 68, but Max moved into a two-shot lead on 141 by the finish of the second round in front of Norman Sutton. A further shot behind were Harry Weetman and Fred Daly. Adams, Bobby Locke, the defending champion, and Peter Thomson, from Australia, were one stroke further back on 145.

After the second round, leading by two shots, Max declared, 'Nobody can catch me now' (he had only 26 putts in his second-round 70 and had made some inspirational shots).

Two rounds were then played on the final day (then played on the Friday, allowing club professionals to tend to their shops) and Max shot a 70 to give himself a six-stroke lead as he went into lunch with Antonio Cerda, his nearest challenger.

Max had come to Portrush in confident mood. According to Henry Longhurst, Max was signing autographs after the second round as 'Open Champion, 1951'. However, it was later revealed that, as Max had made his way to the 1st tee for the final round, he was asked to autograph a golf ball as 'Open Champion'. Years later, he claimed to continue to have nightmares about his seeming arrogance: 'I did put that on a ball when approached by a man and his son before the start of the last round and I had a six-shot lead. I thought, "That's it, I might as well."'

While many winced at Max's seeming lack of humility, Longhurst was possibly correct when he wrote, 'The fates spared him.'

At the long par-4 16th hole of the third round, Max still lead the field by four strokes. He hooked his tee-shot, pulling it badly, just a few inches short of the out-of-bounds fence, close to some steps and barbed wire. He was forced to make a difficult decision: play safe and take a wedge and chip the ball on to the fairway, meaning the likely need to accept a bogey; or he could make a full swing and start the ball out of bounds, hoping to fade it back into play. After protracted experimentation to find a stance which would allow him to strike the ball without gashing his hands on the barbed wire, Max deliberately sliced the ball over the fence with his 3-wood. It obediently turned right, right again and once more right, crossing the fence. The gallery was mesmerised as the ball bounced up the fairway into the heart of the green.

The talkative Frank Stanahan was Max's playing partner. Faulkner had sworn him to unqualified silence, and the American had kept his promise, even declining to return Max's greeting on the 1st tee, until the 16th, when he couldn't help but loudly acclaim, 'That's the greatest shot I've ever seen.'

Max went on to make a third-round 70. However, with the last two rounds, the stress of leading was expected to be too much for a man known more for his salmon-pink plus-twos than Major victories.

Max went to the turn in 37 and dropped shots on the 12th, 15th and 16th.

As he drew his 4-wood to play the approximately 160-yard second shot to the last green, his friend Jimmy Adams, afraid that Max would overhit, attempted to counsel him, letting out a shushing sound. But this only served to distract Max and he hit his ball into the rough to the right of the green, but just in bounds. Fortunately, he was able to get down for a bogey five to win the Championship. Max closed with 74 and a 285 aggregate, three-under-par (this encompassed 102 putts, an average of only 25.5 per round). He recollected the pressure of the final round: 'The last round was a nasty experience. The crowds were rushing everywhere and my caddie was knocked over and both my shoes came off. There was no crowd control as such and, at the 12th, two Irishmen tried to break my nerve. I heard one say to the other for my benefit, "This fellow won't win." Harry Bradshaw was out in 32 and catching up fast.'

The only man left on the course, playing about 45 minutes

behind him, was Cerda, who went out in 34. He reached the 16th tee needing to play the last three holes in 12 strokes to tie with Max – a big ask, that was in the end, too big.

Max's official prize money for winning the Open was £500, and he was paid a similar bonus by the makers of the Dunlop 65 ball he favoured, but, as Max said, 'I made about £12,000 that year. That was pretty good money then.'

Before and throughout the 1951 Championship, Max took walks in the sea to harden his feet. 'I'd go out with my trousers rolled up while the other players were at the bar drinking. I never drank before a big event, but, when I won, I used to get drunk.'

Although a splendid striker of the ball, Max had not been at his best in his iron play at Portrush, and had often looked to his faithful 4-wood. His victory owed much to his majestic touch on the greens. He had recently acquired a new putter with a steel head and a pencil-slim shaft. The fast surfaces at Portrush had suited his style.

Then leaders didn't go out last for the final rounds so Max had an excruciating sojourn in the clubhouse, downing cup after cup of tea, waiting for his rivals to finish.

Cerda approached the final five holes requiring one more birdie to tie, but the Argentinean eventually carded a 70 to leave the Briton the victor by two shots.

Max later said that the victory was all he had ever wanted and that the Open meant everything to him: 'There was no way I was going to lose.'

When he was handed the trophy, Max looked at the names on it – Walter Hagen, Bobby Jones, Gene Sarazen, Sam Snead and

Henry Cotton – and just said to himself 'Wow!' He thought it was marvellous, but in his opinion he had been very lucky.

But his victory wasn't universally celebrated. It seems part of golf's establishment still did not approve of Max Faulkner. For example, Leonard Crawley in the *Daily Telegraph* summed up his 1951 triumph as follows: 'Faulkner is highly strung ... He has tried to hide this very human weakness by dressing himself in gaudy colours and pretending to play the fool as though this were the best way to get on with the job.'

The Open Championship of 1951 was the only one to be played in Ireland to date. British winners, or contenders, were more common in those days; Henry Cotton's last victory had been in 1948. But it took 18 years for another British golfer to emulate Max's success (Tony Jacklin at Royal Lytham in 1969). After the retirement of the 1947 Champion Fred Daly, Max also became the only Open Champion from the British Isles in serious competition.

But that fabulous victory proved to be Max's only Major title, a fact that is hard to understand, given that he was a player of huge ability. Later in life, he tried to explain the underlying cause of his seeming difficulty in realising his potential after Portrush. Max concluded that the victory in 1951 had sapped his will. At the age of 12, he had made a vow to win the Open and, when he finally achieved his ambition as a 34-year-old, on reflection, he thought his desire left him. He had literally done what he had wanted to do.

Max recalled his feelings about defending his title at Lytham, how he had a putt at the 2nd hole of the first round from approximately four feet. After failing to sink the ball, his immediate thought was: 'That's it, I'll never win the Open again.'

He was, of course, sadly right. But there was still a lot of glory to come for the man from Bexhill.

Max was in the Ryder Cup team for Pinehurst in 1951. He was defeated in both his matches; in a singles against Sam Snead, he was four down at lunchtime after scoring 67. In a close match at Wentworth two years later, Max and Dai Rees, who had played in the final of the PGA Match Play Championship (won by Max), were astonished that Henry Cotton, the British captain, failed to ask them to contest the foursomes. At that point, Max had won a suite of tournaments that no other British golfer has succeeded in winning: the Open, the PGA Match Play (1953) and the Dunlop Masters (1951), three of the biggest events on the British circuit, the British Grand Slam, a feat Henry Cotton had never managed.

Max won the Spanish Open Championship three times (he was the last player to win that event two years in succession) and was granted honorary membership of La Puerto de Herro Golf Club, in Madrid, in recognition of this achievement.

In 1952, Max was appointed as the professional at St George's Hill Club, Weybridge and continued to show that independent spirit that endeared him to the crowds but not to some of those that populated the upper echelons of the golf's administration. Peter Alliss recalled a 1954 tour of Argentina, when Max discomfited some of the more sombre members of the party by noisily and repetitively asking, 'Where is this guy Peron?'

TOURNAMENTS AND AWARDS

1937 Berkshire Championship Winner, Addington
    Foursomes

1938 Midland Open Championship

1946 Dunlop – Southport Tournament

1947 West of England Championship

1949 Lotus, Penfold, Dunlop Professional

1950 Winner, Long-Driving Competition, Royal
    Mid-Surrey

1951 British Open, Dunlop Masters; Golf Writers'
    Association Trophy; Winner, Long-Driving
    Competition, Sunningdale; Winner, Long-Driving
    Competition, Brighton; Winner, Long-Driving
    Competition, Bournemouth

1952 Spanish Open, Dunlop Professional; Winner,
    Professional One-Round Tournament, New York

1953 PGA *News of the World* Match Play, Spanish Open

1954 Surrey Open Championship

1957 Spanish Open

1959 Irish Hospitals £5,000

1962 Woodlawn International Tournament,
    West Germany

At Lindrick in 1957, Harry Weetman followed Max's example and withdrew from the singles. As such, the selection for the next day seemed to have been settled affably, and the hullabaloo that followed probably came as something of a surprise to the captain of the Great Britain and Ireland team.

But he had an almost blind faith that the men he had selected to play in the singles would win the day for the home team.

Not long after Rees had swapped the order of play list with the US captain Jack Burke, Weetman purportedly informed a journalist that he would never again play under the captaincy of Rees. When questioned about this, Rees, as might be reasonably expected, was speechless.

Christy O'Connor looked back on events, telling how his captain had opted for a communal selection system among the eight players. On reflection, O'Connor saw this as a bad idea, concluding that Rees should have told the group who was in the team and not asked the players what they thought. For O'Connor, the 'disruptive decision inspired a hell of a rumpus'. This was indirectly because of O'Connor and mostly because of Harry Weetman. There was the hint that, even though O'Connor was the PGA Match Play Champion, he was about to be left out of the team. Bernard Hunt, with forceful backing from Weetman, argued that the Irishman had to be included. Max Faulkner declared openly that he was hitting the ball reasonably well, but putting poorly and that he would not mind being omitted from the next day's play. As Harry Weetman seconded Bernard Hunt's proposal that O'Connor should be in the singles line-up, he conceded that he himself was not playing, or putting too well.

Eric Brown remembered how Dai Rees had tried to engage him in some 'undercover' work over the team selection. But Brown didn't believe that strategic placing of players in a certain order would win matches. He felt that the team should have been treated as being of equal merit and that the opposition needed to be defeated by good golf on the course and not in a team-picking conference.

That evening back in the hotel when Rees announced his singles list, all hell broke loose. Weetman made his statement, and the newspapers swiftly pounced on the juicy story. I'LL NEVER PLAY ON ANOTHER RYDER CUP TEAM CAPTAINED BY DAI REES, screamed the headlines, and extended quotes expressed Weetman's feelings.

Dai and Harry had been travelling companions and friends for a long time and, as the debate widened, Rees declined to comment any further before the conclusion of the match. The whole affair had the feel of an ill-advised newspaper stunt that could have done huge damage to the team spirit of the Great Britain and Ireland side, but the negative press generated by Weetman's comments seemed to bring the home players together in a 'backs to the wall' way and add to their determination to turn things round.

It has been said that Rees suspected that Weetman's reaction had not been something that the Oswestry man had thought up for himself, but that he had been put up to it by 'associates' and family, perhaps including his wife, Freda. As a consequence, in November 1957, Weetman was suspended from PGA events for a year, but the severe penalty was later moderated, partly through the intervention of Rees. However, Harry's banishment from tournament play was estimated to have cost him a potential $84,000 in prize money.

But, as Peter Alliss was to recollect, 'Harry Weetman was furious to be left out. With certain tempers flaring, it didn't augur well for the morrow.'

DAY TWO: 36-HOLE SINGLES

On the morning of the singles, conditions at Lindrick were distinctly different to the first day. The benign course had been dried out by a strong easterly wind. The wind that had changed constantly on the first day got significantly stronger as the second day began. The Britain and Ireland team were heartened, believing that they would be more acclimatised to the blustery conditions. It was clear they would also need to up their playing standards. At least two of the games of the previous day had seen the home team being its own worst enemy.

The USA needed three points from the eight singles matches to retain the Ryder Cup. On six previous occasions, they had achieved the figure with ease, securing the trophy with four singles matches still out on the course.

On the second day, on the instructions of the British PGA, the greens were cut much shorter. Unbelievably, the course green-keeper had thought that the Ryder Cup was due to start a day later than it did, and so the greens at Lindrick on the first day of the Cup had been the usual playing length. With the greens at regulation length, they were quicker and more problematic. As a consequence, six of the USA team required three putts on the 1st green before they became aware of what had happened. With five holes played, the Americans found themselves down in seven games, with the eighth level.

CHAPTER TEN

You Never Had a Hope of Beating Me

TOMMY BOLT (USA)

V

ERIC BROWN (GREAT BRITAIN AND IRELAND)

Looking to answer the US domination of the competition thus far, Dai Rees promoted his Caledonian Rottweiler Eric Brown to meet Tommy Bolt in the opening singles. The American was an opponent for Brown to relish, although the Scot remained calm throughout a tempestuous match.

Tommy Bolt appeared in the Ryder Cup in 1955 and 1957, playing four matches, winning three and losing one. Bolt loved match-play and played well in his two Ryder Cup outings. At Thunderbird Ranch in 1955, he and Jack Burke had a battle royal with Arthur Lees and Harry Weetman. The British pair scored a 68 in the morning round and were just in front by a single hole. Following lunch, they went to the turn in 34 shots and had not bettered their position. Bolt and Burke toiled to be one up with the last hole to play. Weetman holed out for a birdie, but Burke followed him in for a birdie to take the game. In the singles, Bolt had an easy win over Christy O'Connor.

Tommy might be understood as one of the last of the men of his ilk and as a consequence became known as 'Thunder' Bolt. But, like those before him, his tempestuous nature was related to his perfectionism, and, if one of his shots fell short of his expectations, it would send him into a fury. He would snap a club over his knee or hurl it away indiscriminately, or, if his ball had sunk in a lake, the club would also be consigned to Davy Jones's Locker.

However, golf is not a game for the stickler. It is a pursuit in which a 'good bad un' cannot be spurned; the intelligent player looks forward and plots their next shot. However, from Tommy, on many occasions, it brought forth a cavalcade of cussing and a club launched up the fairway. According to Jimmy Demaret, Tommy's putter had spent 'more time in the air than Lindbergh'.

Tommy's uncompromising outlook meant that he was seldom entirely satisfied with a shot. Even after experience and age had mellowed him, Tommy was repeatedly fined by the PGA as a result of his outbursts that, in the past, critics had put down to his lack of 'strength of will' and referred to his displays of emotion as 'gross tantrums' and 'vile behaviour'. Certainly, Tommy's 'expressive nature' attracted publicity. The media legions would follow him through a tournament in the hope of picking up some blue language or an image of a club being hurled into space.

Tommy has been credited with some great one-liners about his attitude to clubs. He has said that, although he did fling the tools of his trade about, he always tried to catch them coming down. He once advised, 'If you are going to throw a club, it is important to throw it ahead of you, down the fairway, so you don't have to waste energy going back to pick it up.'

Another tip was: 'Never break your putter and your driver in the same round or you're dead.'

Numerous tales have evolved around Tommy's antics, and some are more fable than fact. One story that has endured tells of the time Tommy had an argument with his caddie, who had obviously offered an incorrect club for the job that needed doing. The caddie snapped and told Tommy he had no choice and had given him the *one* club left in the bag (the others having been smashed and/or strewn across the greens).

It is a matter of conjecture the number of tournaments Tommy slung away along with his clubs, but according to him his reputation for slinging clubs was exaggerated: 'I threw a couple of clubs … I'm human, like the other guys, but I always threw them at the most opportune time. I always had the camera on me. I never blamed it on anyone but myself – not my caddie, or a camera clicking or the gallery.'

When reminded about the renowned 1960 photograph of him throwing his driver into the lake in front of the 18th tee at Cherry Hills in the US Open won by Arnold Palmer, Tommy insisted that there was a white carp in the lake that had been trying to mess with his game. It seems that, every time he drew back the club, the carp would purposely jump out of the water at the top of his swing. As such, because he was 'provoked', that classic heave didn't count.

In 1957, after a run of poor form, he had decided to take a club-pro job in California. He remembers the year he spent behind that counter as the longest in his life. Treating every member as his boss was one thing, but taking orders from the members' kids was too much for 'Old Dad'. That drove him back to playing, and was motivation enough the following June to achieve his ultimate career goal.

For Tommy, it meant a lot for people to be cheering for him. It inspires him. He once claimed that golfers were really just actors on the course and he saw himself as lucky to be able to perform for the crowds.

Tommy won the 1960 Open by four strokes from the young Gary Player. On a blisteringly hot final day, Tommy played the final two rounds in a brilliant 69 and 72. Remembering that tournament, he said, 'I was probably playing better golf than anybody in the world at that particular time ... I had complete control of my emotions. I birdied the 1st hole, looked back towards the clubhouse and said, "I wonder who's going to finish second?" I know that sounds cocky, but that was the way I felt.'

For all that, Tommy was annoyed when the local press reported his age to be 49, putting a decade on him. When he was told it was a typographical error, Tommy replied, 'Typographical error, my ass ... It was a perfect four and a perfect nine!'

Tommy came late to tournament golf, and he went on the Tour for the first time at the age of 32, in 1950, but the quality and strength of his swing enabled him to extend his career. It took him no time to see himself as being the best player around. His first tournament win came in 1951 in the prestigious North and South Open in Pinehurst, and in most years from then until 1967, when he had nearly reached his half-century, he was included in the top-60 players (those who pre-qualified for tournaments).

Tommy won 15 US Tour events, at least one tournament in every year of the 1950s except for 1959, and, in the 1952 Masters at Augusta, his first, he nearly took another Major. Tommy was level with Sam Snead, the man who would be victorious that year, with four holes to play. On the final four greens, Tommy three-putted three; his putting nerves got the better of him and he finished equal third, five shots behind champion Snead. Looking back, he thought he 'could have won the fucking tournament if I had any sense'. But he saw himself as not having as much desire as he might have, just wanting to be there and be a part of it.

It was in 1955, during the off-season, that Tommy visited Ben Hogan, and he came to see this as the turning-point in his career. Tommy was having trouble with a hook, and Hogan (who had suffered from the same malady early in his career) taught him how to grip the club in order not to hit to the left. Tommy recalled that he went to Hogan and all but got down on his knees for help. The great player told him, 'All you gotta do is move your left hand over to the top of the club.'

Hogan also got him to grip the club in the back three fingers of the left hand and the thumb down the shaft.

According to Tommy, that was when he really started to play golf. He had won tournaments but he didn't know *how* he won them. Looking back, he concluded that it took him around a month of constant practice to get acclimatised to this new grip, but he learned not to fear the hook. Tommy recollected, 'Hogan used to hide behind trees and bushes at Colonial [Country Club in Fort Worth, Texas] as I was working on the change in 1955 to see if I was doing it right. That little son of a bitch helped me … That changed my whole outlook on golf.'

For Tommy, Ben Hogan was his kind of guy. Like Tommy, he had grown up the hard way, with little in the way of money. Hogan had caddied before turning pro, and he was obliged to eat oranges he picked for free from the trees in California before he finally won the North and South at Pinehurst in 1940. Such beginnings contrasted with the likes of Bobby Jones, who Tommy saw as coming from a privileged background. Tommy had dropped out of school in the ninth grade and had to go to work. He believes his knowledge has come by way of experience, not having the education that Bobby Jones could afford.

With his confidence enhanced, Tommy became one of the best ball strikers of all time. His swing was amongst the most respected in the game. He was one of the great characters of post war golf.

Jimmy Demaret, motivated by the late arrival of the belligerent combatants at the tee for the opening singles of the 1957 Ryder Cup, joked that the last time he had seen the pair they were standing at 50 paces, throwing clubs at each other.

Although Brown was full of golfing fire and confident that no American could beat him in a Ryder Cup match, the

Scotsman did not make the best of starts, with his first two shots landing in the rough and sand.

In *Golf Illustrated* (3 October 1957), Henry Cotton wrote,

> I have always had a lot of admiration for Eric Brown, because he is one of those people who has come up the hard way and has retained the courage to call a 'spade a spade' and not be a tiring sort of 'yes man'. He has never had an elegant golf swing; but he has the courage to attack the ball all out, and has learned the hard way, too, that it pays to control the ball through the green.

In the same edition of *Golf Illustrated* in 'Opinion', much was expected of Brown:

> Spearhead of the British side will be the brilliant Scot, Eric Brown, who has just won the Dunlop Masters' Tournament. Although he has been well in the money recently he has not been in first place as often as he has deserved. Now he has received his due reward and we expect to see him at Lindrick in his best fighting form.

Born on Sunday, 15 February 1925 in Edinburgh, Scotland, Eric Chalmers Brown, along with John Panton, dominated Scottish golf in the 1950s. Although the two were unalike in terms of disposition – Brown had an explosive nature, while Panton was a mild-spirited person – they were both fearsome opponents. Brown perhaps had the edge as a competitor as his Ryder Cup record shows (he was unbeaten in all of his four singles games) and he more than once came close to winning the Open Championship.

Unlike many of his professional golfing colleagues, Eric was not born and bred in the vicinity of a course, but he felt that he had his father and mother to thank for his introduction to golf, though neither of his parents had any interest in the sport until after the birth of their third child. They were to become Eric's greatest supporters and his father his most severe critic.

Football might well have been Eric's first sporting love had he lived long enough in the place where he was born, Roseburn Street, which was just a stone's throw from Tynecastle Park, the home of the famous soccer team Heart of Midlothian. Near by, too, is Murrayfield, Scotland's premier rugby ground. Eric was never a rugby fan, but Hearts would always be his team. Eric played quite a lot of football as a youngster and he was a fair player, but golf was his first choice almost as soon as he was able to understand what a golf club was.

Following World War I, George Brown, Eric's father, a wood-carver and cabinet-maker, took a course at a training college and became a technical-subjects teacher. When Eric was just 15 months old, George was employed by a school in Bathgate, a small town halfway between Edinburgh and Glasgow. The new family home in Stuart Terrace lay off the main road; beyond it were the railway line and the local golf course. Because the course was so handy, George thought it made sense to take up golf. Until that point, he knew next to nothing about the game but he became a very keen player. It was not long before Eric's mother also took up the sport. As his father was out all day teaching, and his older brother, Alex, and his sister, Betty, were at school, she took little Eric round the course with her.

Eric never forgot what he called 'those wonderful afternoons', his mother working hard to improve her game and the four-year-old Eric, with a cut-down hickory-shafted club and an old ball, happy to be allowed to do as the adults were doing and over the moon when he hit the ball a dozen yards. The young Brown was learning to swing a club without all the knowledge of detail and method which can hold one back when learning later in life.

But school eventually took up Eric's time and energy. His father, a very strict and determined man, from whom Eric saw himself inheriting a dour character, insisted that education came first and golf second, and, although Eric detested the indoor nature of school, he was obliged to get on with it. Only when school hours were over and at the weekends could he get out to play with his little club of which he was tremendously proud.

Eric looked tough, and he was, and this served him well in the battles of Ryder Cup match-play. His temperament was perfect for the head-to-head encounters, being an inspirational player whose golf could explode into sudden and dazzling life. His record in the singles was outstanding, defeating Lloyd Mangrum, Jerry Barber, Tommy Bolt and Cary Middlecoff. These were mighty opponents, who between them won four US Open Championships, one US PGA Championship and a Masters title.

Eric's Ryder Cup forays started in 1953 at Wentworth with a huge challenge. Alongside John Panton, he was seven holes down at the 9th to Sam Snead and Lloyd Mangrum. The Scotsmen were completely overawed. However, Eric came back in the singles and defeated the tough Mangrum with the help of terrific birdies at the final two holes.

In 1955, at the Thunderbird Club, Eric again lost his foursomes but conquered the diminutive Jerry Barber three and two in their one-to-one encounter.

Eric had watched Bolt play in the Labatt tournament in Canada and had been present for three of the American's club-throwing performances. He remembered in particular the 4th hole where Bolt hurled his driver from the tee after he had hooked into trees and then threw another club, which actually broke, after an unsuccessful attempt to get out on to the fairway. For Eric, club-throwing, so long as it wasn't in the direction of anybody, did no one but the thrower any harm, and even that was a matter of opinion. In fact, Eric saw it as a means of letting off steam and admitted to having thrown a few clubs in his time himself.

Eric later said he saw Bolt as a most pleasant fellow on the first day of the Lindrick match, although Eric thought that the ease with which Bolt and Mayer had defeated Christy O'Connor and himself had something to do with that. But Bolt didn't have much cause for cheerfulness on the second day, as Eric played in a way that did nothing to create a convivial environment for his opponent. A few years on, Eric was recorded as speculating that the American didn't like the 9am early start. Whatever the reason, Bolt seemed to be struggling early on in the match, whereas Eric picked up his game after the first few holes.

The second day's play at Lindrick in 1957 started with the USA taking the opening hole. Eric was fortunate to halve the 2nd, but he swiftly got into his stride and by the 7th had a three-hole lead. Once or twice, Eric found himself having to remind the over-exuberant spectators to keep quiet and still when the American was lining up for a shot, but, at the 9th, after Bolt's second shot had rolled through the green and down a slope into the rough, he angrily suggested to Eric that, if it had been Eric's ball, someone would have kicked it into a good lie! Eric told his opponent to stop moaning.

Eric recalled that, during the first 18 holes, Bolt made some slight mutterings about the crowd being all for the home player. Eric wondered what he expected them to be, though he didn't mention that to Bolt, and, just as Eric had found during 1955 in the United States, many of the spectators were free with their praise for the shots the visitor made as well as those of the home player.

For Eric, the spectators at Lindrick could surely be excused for showing their enthusiasm for a home fight-back. At the same time, as good news of nearly all the Great Britain and Ireland players spread through the crowd, Eric was to recall there had been a great spontaneous cheer from the gallery for Bolt when he holed his chip-shot from behind the 5th green in the afternoon. However, according to Eric, one cannot prevent a golf crowd spotting a player's idiosyncrasies and/or momentary indiscretions, and by the turn in the afternoon they had quite clearly noted Bolt's increasing tendency to grumble about unfavourable lies and bad luck. Probably, too, they had read or heard of his outbursts in his own country.

Playing the 14th, Bolt was still three down. Eric played a bad second there and all of a sudden Bolt was favourite to win the hole, but he was in such a state of temper that he jabbed at a putt of 10 yards and took three to get down. The gallery gloated over the discomfiture of one who, they seemed to think, might crack under any pressure they exerted.

According to Eric, had Bolt not made several fine recovery shots, and had Eric not been only a fraction out with several putts, Bolt would have been in a much more serious position at lunchtime than he actually was; at the end of the morning round, Eric was four holes up, making a determined 71.

Fighting back in typical fashion from the start of the afternoon, Bolt quickly reduced his arrears by 50 per cent. However, the irascible Eric, unleashing the full fury of his attack on his opponent, battled through. But no one could have expected Bolt to make such a mess of the 15th as he did. First, he hooked his drive into the rough, then he made a furious uncontrolled slash which left him still 40 yards short of the 351-yard hole, proceeded to pitch far too strongly, and then overran the hole with his long putt by more than three yards. Eric lay quite close to the hole in two, and Bolt strode up to Eric's ball and, by way of conceding the hole and the match (by a convincing four and three), he swiped the ball right off the green.

The result did much to revive the confidence of the Great Britain and Ireland team. In a dozen Ryder Cups, Great Britain and Ireland had only once before triumphed in the opening singles. While Eric had remained focused, Bolt had putted with difficulty and had found smiling even more of a problem. It had been a cantankerous game and the players both declined to shake hands at the conclusion.

It seems that Eric had won a psychological battle that was started by Bolt. Bolt had appeared to try to slow-play the notoriously speedy Eric. At one point, the Scotsman mysteriously sent his caddie to the clubhouse, but all was revealed when the club carrier soon returned with a lounge chair.

Bolt, like a number of his team-mates, had been displeased by the vocal manner in which the Yorkshire crowds had cheered missed American putts during the foursomes and he continued to complain about the gallery throughout the match. Bolt and the crowd had gone at it from early on and continued an ugly shouting match throughout. He lost control of his emotions, bounced and/or tossed a few clubs and stuck others in the ground. In the future, he would admit, 'You can't play like that.' He lost his concentration and Bolt always believed that 'golf is a game of concentration'.

However, years later, Dow Finsterwald said he was impressed by the way 'God Save the Queen' and 'The Star-Spangled Banner' were greeted. He reflected, 'When a guy misses a putt, they could be applauding the fact that the British team had won a hole. It wasn't maybe the missing of a putt and may have been misinterpreted by some of us.'

It was reported that Bolt smashed a wedge in half in the locker room after the game and grumbled to his team-mate Ed Furgol, 'They cheered when I missed a putt and sat on their hands when I hit a good shot.'

Furgol was pragmatic in reply, telling his compatriot, 'Pipe down – you were well and truly licked.'

Doug Ford was also to reprimand Bolt in the clubhouse for his manner in the face of defeat.

Although he confessed to being very nervous, Bolt later said that he thought that the galleries at Lindrick had, on an individual level, been 'pretty nice folks', and that their collective response was a consequence of the lack of American players competing at the British Open during that era; it was the one chance that British golf fans had to see the best American players. This was certainly the case for the young Tony Jacklin, who would one day win both the US and British Opens. Lindrick is about 60 miles from where he was born, and he still has memories of 1957. He was 13 and he found it unbelievable to be able to see players he'd only read about in magazines.

The US PGA President, Harry Moffitt, had no doubts the crowd was fair: 'When Tommy Bolt's remarks got around, several of the team came to me and said the crowd had been very fair. It had applauded their good shots as well as those of their opponents.'

Moffitt further discounted Bolt's remarks by recalling that the man from Oklahoma had previously threatened to quit a match with Sam Snead, having heard the crowd was rooting for Snead against him.

For all this, 'Thunder' Bolt said he had not taken much pleasure from the match, and snarled at Eric, 'You won, Eric, but I didn't enjoy the game.'

Eric allegedly answered, 'No, of course you didn't enjoy it

because you were fucking licked … you knew when the games were drawn that you never had a hope of beating me.'

The Scot also told his vanquished rival that he could expect the same medicine any time in the future.

Eric was to consider that he might have been unlucky in the types of player he met in Ryder Cup singles; however, he could say without boasting that he had bettered them in more respects than one.

Tom Scott in *Golf Illustrated* (10 October 1957) wrote,

It was a pity that defeat was sour in the mouth of one of the United States team, and that the British spectators were pilloried by as poor a sportsman as has played golf in these islands.

I have been asked: Did the spectators loudly applaud good British shots and stay silent at good American ones? The answer is 'No'. What they did do was to applaud good British shots more loudly than good American ones. But with the rising tension and a great British victory in sight was that to be wondered at? But it is not true to say they 'sat on their hands' when the Americans sent a good one towards the pin.

Then on the greens after an American missed a putt there was a few moments' silence, then as the players started to walk off the green there was applause. Anything wrong with that?

I think a defence to Bolt's accusations has to be written and written quickly before he spreads the poison as quickly as he can.

Having written these words let us forget the sourness of one man and only remember the skill and determination of our winning side.

The acrimonious opening encounter was to set the tone for what remained of the match.

HOLE BY HOLE – MATCH ONE																				
Players	**1**	**2**	**3**	**4**	**5**	**6**	**7**	**8**	**9**	**Out**	**10**	**11**	**12**	**13**	**14**	**15**	**16**	**17**	**18**	**In**
Bolt	4	4	4	5	4	4	5	4	4	38	4	3	3	5	4	4	4	4	4	37 75
Brown	5	4	3	4	4	3	4	4	4	35	4	4	3	4	5	4	5	3	3	36 71
Bolt	4	4	4	5	3	3	4	4	4	35	4	4	3	4	5	5				Won 4 & 3
Brown	6	4	4	4	4	X	3	4	4	-	5	3	4	4	5	4				

CHAPTER ELEVEN

Mills on Fire

Jack Burke (USA)
V
Peter Mills (Great Britain and Ireland)

The only rookie on the Great Britain and Ireland team was Peter Mills. He was looked upon as possibly a weak link in the side, but he played quite beautifully. Along with Harry Bradshaw, he had been brought in to replace Max Faulkner and Harry Weetman in the singles. He had been scheduled to meet Ted Kroll, but sickness prevented the American from playing. Although Rees might have claimed a point for a forfeited game, in a magnanimous sporting spirit, Dai agreed to Jack Burke, who had previously withdrawn himself from the singles, stepping into the breach. This was a particularly munificent gesture as Burke was acknowledged to be the best American player on the US team and it was widely thought that Mills would be little more than cannon fodder in the face of the biggest gun the visitors had in their armoury. However, Mills was to be the David to Burke's Goliath.

Peter Mills was born on 6 June 1931. He achieved several second places in tournaments in the 1950s, but for a player with a fine swing it was surprising that Mills did not play more than his single Ryder Cup game.

In what was the encounter of the 'substitutes', Burke, undefeated in Ryder Cup matches, three-putted the 1st green and lost the hole. Mills kept hitting the ball down the middle, leaving Burke to make the mistakes, and he made plenty! The Pinner Hill professional surprised everyone by taking an early four-up lead on his vastly more experienced opponent. Burke hit a mournfully poor 77 in the morning, leaving him five holes adrift of doughboy Mills at lunch. He had putted poorly, but Jack won the 200-yard 18th with a bogey four, so saving him going into lunch six down.

In the afternoon, the 1956 United States PGA Champion fought back, but was unable to catch the debutant, who achieved one of the biggest upsets in the history of the Ryder Cup, winning five and three, levelling the match at 3–3 and hoisting his side's morale sky high. The great cheer coming across the course told everyone that a second singles home win had been achieved.

The defeat was Burke's only loss in the eight matches he played in the Ryder Cup. As such, coming in as a late replacement, perhaps without due preparation and possibly underestimating his opponent, meant that Burke had probably sacrificed a place among the great heroes of the Ryder Cup.

Although Mills was chosen to play in the Ryder Cup of 1959, injury prevented him from taking part. He was never to make the team again and as such finished his Ryder Cup career with a 100 per cent record: played one, won one.

HOLE BY HOLE – MATCH TWO																				
Players	1	2	3	4	5	6	7	8	9	Out	10	11	12	13	14	15	16	17	18	In
Burke	5	4	3	4	5	4	5	4	5	39	5	2	4	4	5	5	6	4	3	37 75
Mills	4	4	4	4	5	3	4	3	4	35	4	3	4	4	5	4	5	4	4	36 71
Burke	4	4	3	4	4	3	4	4	5	35	4	3	4	4	4	C				Won 5 & 3
Mills	4	4	3	5	4	3	5	3	5	36	4	4	4	4	4	X				

bove: Great Britain's Max Faulkner was a fine golfer who won almost
ery major British Championship.

elow: USA team members Doug Ford, Fred Hawkins and Ed Furgol
rriving for a practice session.

Above: Great Britain and Ireland's Christy O'Connor, considered a natural golfer and ranked amongst the finest players ever produced by Ireland.

Below: USA's Ed Furgol: 'My luck is so bad that, if I bought a cemetery, people would stop dying.'

Above: Great Britain's Eric Brown, a distinguished match-player who was quite inspirational in his singles win over Tommy Bolt.

Below: Great Britain's Ken Bousfield plays out of a bunker at the 5th in one of the opening matches.

Right: USA's Ted Kroll, a highly successful foursomes player with a fantastic swing.

Below: USA's Jack Burke Jr, the US captain in 1957 and a golf legend. 'If the British team comes back and wins this, you can bury me under 10 tons of compost.'

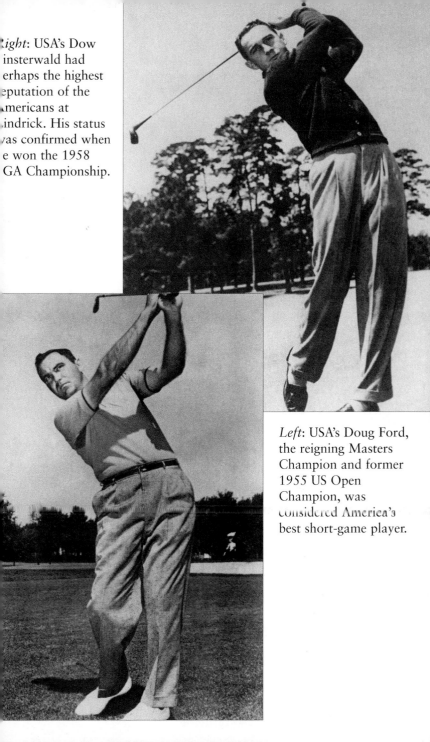

Right: USA's Dow
Finsterwald had
perhaps the highest
reputation of the
Americans at
Lindrick. His status
was confirmed when
he won the 1958
PGA Championship.

Left: USA's Doug Ford,
the reigning Masters
Champion and former
1955 US Open
Champion, was
considered America's
best short-game player.

Left: USA's Lionel Hebert won six PGA Tour titles during his career.

Right: USA's Tommy Bolt, a fearsome-as-thunder character, who was a golfer of the highest class.

Above: Great Britain's Max Faulkner, sometimes referred to as 'Mighty Max'.

Below left: Great Britain's Peter Alliss was still on the course when the match result was decided.

Below right: Great Britain's Harry Weetman, one of the finest pitchers in Britain.

Left: Dai Rees congratulates Ken Bousfield who putted like an angel to give Great Britain the vital 7th point, the one that would win the Ryder Cup.

Below: Great Britain's Dai Rees celebrates. Few golfers have given themselves with such passion and resolve to the British cause in the Ryder Cup as Dai Rees who played in nine Ryder Cups.

CHAPTER TWELVE

Alliss in Wonder Land

FRED HAWKINS (USA)

V

PETER ALLISS (GREAT BRITAIN AND IRELAND)

Just before the singles matches got under way, Peter Alliss remembered how Dai Rees went round his team saying that the singles draw had worked out very well for Great Britain and Ireland. He told Alliss that he would have no trouble at all in disposing of Fred Hawkins, 'the weakest man on their team'. That sounded familiar to Peter as it echoed something said to him in 1953. As Alliss began his singles game, in his words, 'The iron men of America first faltered.'

After the first 18 holes, almost all the Great Britain and Ireland team were up, and in the afternoon the cheering was particularly loud from around the turn as American after American went down, often by almost unbelievable margins. The crowds were running wild, sensing victory.

At the age of 22, in 1953, Alliss had become the youngest player to be selected for the Ryder Cup and he was the first son to follow his father into a Ryder Cup team. At that point, he had yet to win an important professional tournament.

The young Alliss was perhaps a victim of his own sensibilities; he dwelt on his inability to hole a putt on Wentworth's last green in his 1953 Ryder Cup match and could not recover. The opportunity for a British victory over the Americans had depended on him and Bernard Hunt, both of whom were Ryder Cup virgins. It fell to them to play the last matches on the course on the final day. If both of them could have achieved a par 5 down the 18th, it would have brought the Cup home. Each player took six. Alliss took four shots when only about 40 yards from the hole. Hunt halved his match, but Alliss was beaten by Jimmy Turnesa; Alliss was near to tears as he shook hands with the American, having lost by one hole.

Alliss was never to forget that experience or the vitriol the press let loose on the two young men the next day. Alliss was adamant in his conviction that he was passed over for the 1955 encounter with the Americans (along with Hunt) because of his failure two years before, despite having won the 1955 Dunlop Masters, the last tournament before the final selection was made.

His opponent, Fred Hawkins, born on 3 September 1923, was a very consistent player on the American Tour, but this would be his only Ryder Cup appearance. From 1949 to 1963, he usually finished in the top 25 and often in the top 10. However, he won just one PGA event, the Oklahoma City Open in 1956.

At Lindrick in 1957, the Alliss v Hawkins game was the

only singles match in which the home side was to find itself behind following the initial nine holes. After six, Alliss was three down, but he won eight, nine and ten to pull level.

With the morning done, Hawkins was a hole up. He rapidly improved his advantage after the break to put himself three in front.

Over six holes, Alliss replied with a further series of four wins and for the first time took the lead. With 10 played, Alliss was one up. He needed to drop a 15-foot putt to halve the 11th in birdie twos.

At the 13th, then a par 5 of 470 yards, Alliss looked likely to go further ahead until Hawkins holed a long putt for a half in four.

Hawkins made a birdie four on the long 14th. At the 16th, 486 yards, the American went ahead with another birdie but faltered at the 17th, a par 4 of 387 yards, when he was short in two. It was at this point Alliss remembers having the match lost for him. Peter and Hawkins were at the height of their battle and the match finely balanced. As Allis prepared to play his own shot to the green, Dai Rees and Ken Bousfield came running up. 'It doesn't matter,' Dai said, 'we've won, we've won ... relax, we've won ... don't worry.'

But, for Alliss, after his 1953 fiasco and the consequent fall-out, it *did* matter; as he was to say, it mattered 'a helluva lot to me'.

But the news of the team's overall victory took all the stuffing out of Alliss. He was highly delighted; however, the information did nothing for his concentration and he sent his second shot under a hedge to the right of the green. Alliss could do no better than six and Hawkins had only to make a five to win the hole and the match two and one.

Hawkins's glee was palpable, but his satisfaction with his personal accomplishment was short-lived as he became aware of the devastation that was being wrought on his team as he struggled with Alliss. He said later, 'I was concentrating on my match with Alliss and thought we were winning.'

HOLE BY HOLE – MATCH THREE																			
Players	1	2	3	4	5	6	7	8	9	Out	10	11	12	13	14	15	16	17	18	In
Hawkins	4	4	3	5	3	3	4	4	5	35	5	3	4	4	4	4	5	5	3	36 71
Alliss	4	4	4	6	4	3	4	3	4	36	4	3	4	4	4	4	6	5	3	36 72
Hawkins	4	4	3	3	5	3	5	5	4	36	5	2	4	4	4	4	4	W		Won 2 & 1
Alliss	4	4	5	4	4	3	4	4	4	36	4	2	4	4	5	4	5	C		

CHAPTER THIRTEEN

Putting Like an Angel

LIONEL HEBERT (USA)

V

KEN BOUSFIELD (GREAT BRITAIN AND IRELAND)

Lionel P Hebert was born on 20 January 1928 in Lafayette, Louisiana, and was a fearsome opponent for Ken Bousfield. The American had won five times on the US PGA Tour, including the 39th PGA Championship in 1957 at Miami Valley in Dayton, Ohio, the last to be organised as a match play event. In the final, Hebert went up by a hole on Dow Finsterwald with a birdie at the 32nd hole, then closed the match and the Championship with a routine par at the 35th, winning two and one. Lionel's older brother, Jay, would win the same – then stroke-play – event at Firestone Country Club in Akron, Ohio, in 1960, beating Australian Jim Ferrier (281(1)). Both Jay and Lionel attended Louisiana State University, where Lionel graduated with a degree in music.

Lionel became a professional golfer in 1950, and the 1957 Ryder Cup was the only time he was selected for the competition.

His opponent Ken Bousfield's great strengths were his putting, and his short game, which in general was superb being based on his slow even tempo that he maintained under even the most severe pressure. He was a fine player of all kinds of wedge shots, particularly the pitch and run.

Dick Burton, British Open Champion of 1939 (played over the Old Course at St Andrews in Scotland) and Great Britain Ryder Cup player (1935, 1937, 1949), said of Bousfield, 'Within 100 yards of the hole, I have never seen anyone better.'

This skilful touch compensated for his relative lack of length and he was at his best on fast-running courses when refinement and control, rather than power, were needed.

Bousfield won a Dunlop tournament at Southport and Ainsdale in 1957 with a brilliant exhibition of golf; he did not take more than five shots for any hole over five rounds. It was also in 1957 that Ken won the Belgian Open. In 1958, his final round of 66 at Crans-sur-Sierre in the Swiss Open, completing the last nine holes in 30 strokes, gave him victory by one shot over the great Belgian Flory van Donck, at that time considered the greatest golf player ever produced by Continental Europe. Van Donck was renowned for his putting, though his style was unconventional, as he kept the toe of his putter in the air (not unlike Isao Aoki).

Van Donck won his own national title 16 times between 1935 and 1968, and held most of the national titles in Europe at one time or another, including the Dutch Open (1936, 1937, 1951, 1953), the French Open (1954, 1957, 1958), the German Open (1953, 1956) and the Swiss Open (1953, 1955). He was second in the British Open in 1956 and 1959.

Bousfield had two top-10 finishes at the Open Championship, tying for fifth in 1955 and eighth in 1961.

At Lindrick in 1957, Ken Bousfield had given himself a four-hole safety margin by the 9th. At the conclusion of the morning's play, he had pushed the gap to five, courtesy of a splendid lengthy birdie putt, struck from the backend of the 18th green.

Following the recommencement of play, Bousfield extended his lead to seven. At this point, Hebert seemed to realise his back was most definitely to the proverbial wall, and initiated blistering retaliation, taking three holes in succession and it seemed that Bousfield was about to collapse under the strain. But Max Faulkner and Dai Rees had hurtled through the crowd to let Bousfield know the state of play, and that the Great Britain and Ireland team needed his point.

The plucky Englishman responded. He held off the onslaught and struck an enchanting chip on to the 8th green to set up an eight-foot putt that he sank with ease to return to five up.

Hebert, six down at the turn, attempted another counterattack. He won two holes, but, with the 15th halved, Bousfield was left to make an 18-inch putt to take the game for four and one. This was the vital seventh point, the one that would win the Ryder Cup.

Hebert admitted that his Brit opponent had 'putted me off the course'.

According to Ken Bousfield, 'I was driving like an idiot and putting like an angel.'

Later comparing this momentous triumph with the 1985 victory won by Sam Torrance over Andy North, Ken said, 'The one big difference from Torrance's was that my match finished out in the country, on the 15th green. But it wasn't the same sort of emotion. I can understand Sam crying. I didn't in 1957 – but I felt like it.'

HOLE BY HOLE – MATCH FOUR																				
Players	1	2	3	4	5	6	7	8	9	Out	10	11	12	13	14	15	16	17	18	In
Hebert	5	5	4	4	5	3	5	4	5	40	5	3	4	4	5	4	5	4	3	37 77
Bousfield	4	5	4	4	4	3	4	4	4	36	4	3	5	5	5	3	4	4	2	36 72
Hebert	5	4	3	5	4	2	4	4	5	36	4	4	4	4	5	4				Won 4 & 3
Bousfield	5	4	2	4	5	3	5	3	4	35	5	4	4	4	5	5	4			

CHAPTER FOURTEEN

Never Say Dai

ED FURGOL (USA)

V

DAI REES (GREAT BRITAIN AND IRELAND)

It was something of a mystery how Edward Joseph Furgol, born on 22 March 1917, in New York Mills, New York, was able to swing a golf club with any art whatsoever, given that, as a 12-year-old, he shattered his left elbow in an accident falling from playground crossbars. It had been badly set and his left arm was bent stiff at the elbow and withered. That arm was never much use in the swing except to help Ed to guide the club. But he found ways to manage the problem. For instance, he built up the left-hand grip on his clubs to tennis-racket width, and compensated for his short swing by lunging powerfully through the ball. However, it has to be said that, in a game which stresses the straight left arm, Ed proved that it is the hands which swing and that the spirit can overcome physical limitations. As a man who has often been quoted as saying, 'My luck is so bad that, if I bought a cemetery, people would stop dying,' Ed did much to overcome ill fortune.

Ed grew up in Utica, in the State of New York. Known as 'The City that God Forgot', Utica is one of a number of industrial towns and cities in the northeastern 'Rust Belt'. Utica was ruled by the Democratic Party for nearly half a century following World War II. Although the city had numerous mayors in the post-war period, the real boss of the metropolis was Rufus Elefante, although he never held elected political office. Elefante and his cronies ran almost every aspect of business in Utica from Marino's restaurant, deriving power from the city's large Italian-American immigrant population. The Italians received political favours from Elefante (via his 'servants' in city government) in exchange for their block vote to back up the mobster's wishes. At one time, Utica was commonly referred to as 'Sin City'.

It was in this unlikely context that Ed had his earliest dreams of being a champion golfer. Regardless of his handicap, Ed continued to pursue golf through the pain of stretching, working as a caddie and swinging with his 'problematic' arm and he built the capacity to strike the ball very forcefully to become one of the leading American amateurs. In 1938, he entered the Amateur Public Links Championship (APLC) and finished second, behind Detroit's Walter Burkemo (Walter, one of 13 children, would be the 1953 PGA Champion). Many other graduates of the Public Links Championship have gone on to greater glory in golf.

In 1940, Ed was back at the APLC in Detroit, representing Utica. He tied for the qualifying medal with a then record 138 for 36 holes and played through four matches to the semi-finals, where he lost on the 38th hole to the eventual champion, Robert Clark, of St Paul.

Ed won the North and South Amateur event in 1945 and joined the professional ranks soon after this success.

Ed's best year was 1954; he was victorious in two tournaments, one of which was the US Open at the Baltusrol Club, Springfield, New Jersey. Regarded by many as little more than a journeyman, Ed had just settled down as a club professional after 10 years on the PGA Tour. There was something to this rather limited analysis of Ed's career, but, as Ed himself pointed out, 'Club pro? I'm a club pro *and* a playing pro! I have an average of 71.5 strokes for more than a thousand rounds of golf on the circuit in the last 10 years.'

For all this, Ed's victory at Baltusrol shook the world of golf and made Open history.

On three previous occasions, Ed had qualified for the final 36 holes in the Open. The last time had been in 1949, but his best previous effort was a tie for 12th place in 1946, when he had 77-69-74-69-289.

Billy Joe Patton of Morgantown, North Carolina, an amateur, led on the first day with a 69, and remained a threat throughout, but, coming from the Westwood Country Club, St Louis, Missouri, Ed played with focus and determination over the Lower Course. He scored 71-70-71-71-284, four over par, staying just ahead of the 23-year-old Gene Littler, from San Diego, California, the 1953 Amateur Champion who had turned professional just the previous January (three months after his Amateur success). Littler, of course, would win the

US Open in 1961. One of a new breed of college-educated golfers, Littler would be in the American Ryder Cup teams of 1961, 1963, 1965, 1967, 1969, 1971 and 1975, and had a 14-5-8 win/loss/tie record including five wins and three ties in 10 singles matches.

When Ed came out for the third round of the Open Championship, he was tied with Ben Hogan for second place with a 36-hole score of 141, two strokes behind the leader Littler. Going into the final day, Hogan was looking for his fifth Open victory, but he took 76 for his third round and finished in a tie for sixth at 289.

The final hole in the last round over Baltusrol's superb Lower Course, was a great tester for the front runners. This 18th hole was 54 yards long. The drive was downhill, with a brook, rough and trees to the left and goodly rough and more trees on the right. It was a tight tee-shot. The second shot swung uphill to the left, across the curling brook, but the green was within range of the second shot for many players. Dick Mayer came to the final hole needing a par 5 for a 72-hole score of 284. Instead, his drive found an unplayable lie under an evergreen, and Dick took seven.

Ed was next and drove in among the trees on the left. Seeing he had no shot at the fairway on the Lower Course, Ed pitched out on to the 18th fairway of Baltusrol's Upper Course, and pitched his third to the front apron of the green. He chipped six feet past the hole. If Ed had failed to hole that putt for a par 5, it would have changed the entire outcome of the event, as later Littler hit his second shot towards the 18th green and had the hard luck to see his ball catch a bunker at the left. His effort to extract himself worked excellently but he was left eight feet short. Had he holed the putt, he would have tied with Ed's 284. If Mayer had taken a par 5 or if Ed had missed his six-foot putt or if Littler had holed his eight-footer, there might have been another name on the trophy in 1954. But Furgol made his par 5 and won very positively. He finished one stroke better than Littler.

Sportswriter Arthur Daley wrote of Furgol's victory, 'Ed Furgol won it. What more can anyone ask?'

That year was a record-breaking one: the prize money, originally fixed at approximately $20,000, was increased several days before play began by a 20 per cent bonus for each prize. The total actually awarded was $23,280, a new USGA record, with the winner receiving $6,000, of which Ed passed $1,050 to his caddie.

The entry was 1,928 (the former record was 1,688 in 1952) and the gallery hit 39,600, the biggest ever. The event was televised from coast to coast for the first time – NBC produced a two-hour telecast on the last day. Another first in a USGA Championship of that year was that every fairway was fully roped from tee to green.

Accepting his prize, Ed said, 'I only hope I can give something back to golf.'

In 1955, Ed and Chick Harbert represented the USA in the Canada Cup (which had started two years earlier). Their victory was the first of America's 22 wins in the 20th century.

In 1956, Ed won two more events, claimed fourth place in the US Open and reached the semi-finals of the US PGA Championship.

Ed won another event in 1957, the Agua Caliente Open, before slowly withdrawing from tournament play to concentrate on his role as a club professional.

Up in all but one match, with the usual US singles haul muted, as his singles game in the 1957 Ryder Cup got under way, Dai Rees was conscious that his team might be on the brink of a momentous result and that 1957 might finally be the year that the Ryder Cup would be taken from what had become its American domicile. Seemingly inspired by the unfolding events, he laid into Furgol like an avenging Druid warrior, taking just 33 strokes to smash through the opening nine holes; this was the best performance of the day. A rip-roaring birdie at the par-3 18th meant that the Welshman was four up going into lunch.

Furgol appeared to have no adequate response as, during the subsequent period, beginning with a triplet of threes, Rees amassed a seven-hole lead at the turn and maintained his mastery of the American to finish the seven and six winner, leaving Furgol reeling. However, to be fair, it is likely that Rees would have beaten anyone in the world on that particular day and the American stood no chance against such a determined will to win.

As was fitting, captain Rees played the best golf of the day, taking maximum points from the games he had contested. Both times he was out in 33 and, in the troublesome conditions, that was golf of the very highest class.

Appreciating that victory was now possible, the home skipper quickly shook hands with Furgol, then sped off around Lindrick in the hope of inspiring his men in the final three matches to bring the Ryder Cup back across the Atlantic.

Three matches had been won by Great Britain and Ireland and only two and a half more points were needed to win the Cup. By now, hundreds of people had gathered round the giant scoreboard to watch Eddie Carter (who would become the Recorder of the European PGA Tour when it started in 1972) put up the hole-by-hole scores. The two vital matches, ones which had worried most of the home supporters at lunchtime, were those involving Hunt and O'Connor.

HOLE BY HOLE – MATCH FIVE																			
Players	1	2	3	4	5	6	7	8	9	Out	10	11	12	13	14	15	16	17	18	In
Furgol	4	4	4	5	4	3	4	4	4	36	4	3	4	5	W	3	5	5	C	
Rees	4	4	3	4	4	2	5	3	4	33	5	3	4	4	C	3	5	4	W	
Furgol	5	4	3	6	6	3	4	4	4	39	4	4	5							Won 7 & 6
Rees	3	3	3	4	4	3	5	4	4	33	5	4	4							

CHAPTER FIFTEEN

Are You Sick, Doug?

DOUG FORD (USA)

V

BERNARD HUNT (GREAT BRITAIN AND IRELAND)

Between 1953 and 1969, Bernard Hunt represented Great Britain and Ireland in the Ryder Cup in eight out of nine tournaments, a tremendously long career in the competition. He won six times, lost 16 and halved six, but as a singles player he lost just three times in 10 matches and he was victorious on four occasions.

Hunt's first appearance in the Ryder Cup had not been memorable and he was to admit that he 'made a bit of pig's ear of it'. Partnering Jimmy Adams in the foursomes, he suffered as Ted Kroll and Jack Burke pulled seven holes ahead by lunchtime. On the second day, the result of the whole match depended on the inexperienced and youthful shoulders of Hunt and Peter Alliss, who messed up on the 36th hole to lose his match.

However, if Hunt could win against Dave Douglas, it would

have at least forced the first tie in Ryder Cup history. Hunt struggled against Douglas but pulled it back to all square on the 16th. Douglas then knocked two balls out of bounds on the 17th and, although Hunt had lost count of how many shots his opponent had taken, he ignored the referee's advice to pick his ball up and instead waited for the formal concession.

Hunt was one up on the 36th tee, and was pretty confident that, with a par 5, he would beat the American. But, as he said himself, 'Then I went and mucked up 18 to halve the match.'

He was short of the green in two shots, over-hit a run-up shot to the green and needed three putts, which gave the Americans a narrow victory. Alliss and Hunt were subsequently left out of the 1955 Ryder Cup team. But Bernard had a good year anyway, getting married to his wife Margaret, with whom he has three children.

In 1957, playing behind Rees, Hunt was attempting to redeem himself against the formidable Doug Ford, who was reputed to be invincible in match-play, and America's best short-game player, for the defeat at Wentworth two years earlier.

Ford played in four Ryder Cup teams: 1955, 1957, 1959 and 1961, winning four matches, losing four and tying one. He began his run in the Cup with two wins at Thunderbird Ranch in 1955.

From the start of his career, it was obvious that Ford liked to play fast and was capable of incredible accuracy from just off the green. He had a gift that is seen rarely in any generation. It was said that not since Johnny Revolta (who had roamed the fairways a quarter of a century before Ford) had there been a player who could get down in two as often from within 100 yards of the hole as Ford.

Gifted with a sense of humour and a way with words, in the 1957 Pensacola tournament, Ford teed off in the third round and shot a remarkable 45 on the first nine holes. Everyone was stunned. He was asked, 'Are you sick, Doug?'

Ford replied, 'Heck no. I'm all right. It's just that I stubbed my toe on the television set last night.'

He then hit a 68 in the final round to finish in the money.

Facing Ford in the 1957 singles, Bernard Hunt was apparently undaunted by the American sinking the longest of long putts on the 7th, 8th and 9th; at the turn, the Englishman was one in front and had maintained this lead at the halfway point.

In the second session against Ford at Lindrick, battling Bernard stormed the front nine holes. He won five holes, only losing the 6th to an aggressive birdie two by the wounded Ford; Hunt was out in 32.

Trailing by five with three-quarters of the match played, deadly Doug could not respond to Hunt's blitz and surrendered on the 13th, reeling on the end of the six and five bashing.

At this point, Harry Bradshaw was tied with Dick Mayer with only four holes to play, while out on the 15th green Ken Bousfield was about to beat Lionel Hebert.

Bradshaw and Alliss were the only Great Britain and Ireland players still on the course when the match result was decided.

HOLE BY HOLE – MATCH SIX																			
Players	**1**	**2**	**3**	**4**	**5**	**6**	**7**	**8**	**9**	**Out**	**10**	**11**	**12**	**13**	**14**	**15**	**16**	**17**	**18**	**In**
Ford	5	4	4	4	4	3	4	3	4	35	4	4	5	4	3	4	5	5	5	39 74
Hunt	5	3	3	4	4	3	4	4	4	34	5	5	3	4	4	4	5	4	3	37 71
Ford	5	4	3	5	C	2	5	3	4	-	5	4	5	4						Won 6 & 5
Hunt	4	4	3	4	4	2	4	3	3	32	5	4	4	4						

154

CHAPTER SIXTEEN

If You Can't Outplay Them, Outwork Them

Dow Finsterwald (USA)

V

Christy O'Connor (Great Britain and Ireland)

Christy O'Connor had been matched against America's 'young buck' Dow Finsterwald. Finsterwald, then aged 27 against the Irishman's 32, had come to Lindrick nominated as the best young prospect of the time on the US Tour.

It was just five years after he bought a set of World Series clubs that he let the golf world know he was a rising power in the game. While still in college at Ohio University, and thus an amateur, he shot a 61 in a round of the St Louis Open in 1950. At the time, it was the lowest single-round score ever posted in the PGA, though the record stood for only five months. A year later, he became a professional. His first win came in 1955 and, shortly before Lindrick, he was the runner-up to Lionel Hebert in the US PGA Match Play Championship of 1957 (by two and one). He followed this up by winning the Vardon Trophy.

Although sometimes characterised as a very cautious player, Finsterwald was renowned for his shot-making abilities. His skill with the short game especially drew rave reviews. Looking back on his career, he recalled how he hit a lot of balls (on the practice range), but he enjoyed doing it. It was often said that he was a tireless worker, but for Finsterwald it was his love of the game that brought success; he just didn't consider it work. He remembered that *Time* magazine once had Ben Hogan on the cover, and quoted the great man as saying, 'If you can't outplay them, outwork them.' He took the advice, but this never detracted from his enjoyment of just playing that enabled him to finished fifth or better more than 50 times.

In 1956, Finsterwald had finished second-highest money-winner in America and, as he walked out to face O'Connor, he was third in the money list, adding to his runner-up prize in the American PGA Championship, by matching that position in three other major Tour events.

But reputations meant little to O'Connor: 'When I climb up on to the 1st tee, I regard my chances as at worst 50–50 against any opponent. The ballyhoo surrounding Finsterwald merely strengthened my resolve.'

O'Connor didn't play tournament golf in Britain before 1954, when he was almost 30 years old. His relatively late arrival on the British scene implies that O'Connor was a late developer, but, in fact, he was not able to afford the cost of playing in Britain before the mid-1950s. On 12 October that year, he married Mary Collins from Tuam, County Galway, and, as he and his wife walked down the aisle Mary said, 'We have no money.'

Her new husband responded, 'Don't worry. I'll win it and you can mind it.'

He was as good as his word. O'Connor began his assault on the European circuit. The couple honeymooned at the Gleneagles Hotel in Scotland, where Christy won his first tournament outside Ireland.

In 1955, the Bundoran Club paid his expenses to the Swallow Penfold tournament, which he won, taking the first ever £1,000 prize in Europe, and in that same year Christy played at Thunderbird Ranch in his first Ryder Cup.

As O'Connor practised with Harry Bradshaw, the Irish pairing looked like a natural selection for the foursomes, but captain Dai Rees decided against this and didn't play O'Connor until the second day when he was lead-off man in the singles against the aggressive Tommy Bolt. This was, to say the least, a baptism of fire for O'Connor, who was obliged to cope with Bolt's infamous thunderous temper and a caddie who seemed intent on doing all he could to help the USA win. O'Connor recollected, 'It was my first visit to the United States and I tended to rely more on my caddie's club selection rather than my own instincts.'

O'Connor had been convinced that he could match Bolt. But, early on in the 36-hole game, he fell behind. However, at the 6th, it seemed he might pull one back as Tommy had got himself stranded in a bunker. At the centre of the fairway, the Galway man's caddie passed him a 3-iron; O'Connor made a flawless connection and expected to make the putting surface. He was amazed as the ball flew over the green to land in a bush. Looking back, he remembered, 'I had been fooled. I was badly misclubbed and now I had lost a hole. I should have won … As we progressed, the clubbing got worse and, when we arrived at the 18th green, I was three down.'

Going in to lunch, O'Connor told his caddie he didn't want any more of his advice on club selection. Working with his own intuition, he made a good start to the second 18 and soon was just one down. In the face of the increasing pressure, errors began to infect Bolt's play and the clubs started to fly. It looked as if O'Connor had broken his opponent. But, with the helpful advice and counselling of Phil Harris, the multitalented musician, comedian and orchestra leader, an old friend of Bolt's, the American began to regain his focus, and won four and two.

His debut in the Cup concluded as a mixed experience for O'Connor. He appreciated the chance to pit himself against the Americans in their own backyard, but what he saw as the seemingly defeatist attitude of the Great Britain and Ireland side didn't sit well with him. It was a mentality that he continued to experience throughout his career as a Ryder Cup player. According to O'Connor, the feeling that prevailed for many years was that the USA could not be beaten and that all that could be expected of him and his team-mates was to play the best they could. He stopped short of condemning the captains of the time, but he believed they should have been stronger willed and in control of the team, telling the players, 'Let's go out and win', rather than what became a traditional: 'Let's go out and put up a good show.'

The pillar of O'Connor's game was his silky swing, which he performed with a flowing rhythmic grace. The golfing immortal Lee Trevino once said of O'Connor, 'To me, only three players have looked entirely natural swinging a golf club – Christy, Roberto de Vicenzo and Neil Coles. Christy flows through the ball like fine wine.'

His fellow professionals knew O'Connor as 'Wristy Christy' because he was able to hit the ball with a definite flick of the wrists. He was seen as a 'natural' golfer, but that magnificently open and unrestrained action had been entrenched by repeated and extensive practice, particularly, in his early years, on the sands of his Galway home. He was a robust, attacking golfer, who was able to conceive of a staggering variety of shots, perhaps a greater range than any player of his time, having the ability to invent shots to get himself out of trouble.

Norman Drew, one of a select band to have played in the Walker Cup, the Ryder Cup and the World Cup, said of Christy, 'He was a genius with a wedge in his hands … as a rough-weather player, he had few equals and I remember, when we had a ballot on the best "escape artist" in Europe, he won by a mile.'

There is one particular tale that illustrates O'Connor's ability as a shot-maker. He was involved in a practice round with a rookie professional. The young man smashed an 8-iron on to the green of a par 3. O'Connor replied by floating in a 5-iron. His companion noticed that an 8-iron was all he had required. The Irishman gave an impromptu exhibition, using every club in his bag, from putter to driver, to hit the green. In this remarkable demonstration, O'Connor displayed a panoply of skills – from toeing in the pitching irons and avoiding the loft by hitting with the hands well ahead of the club head at impact, to floating in high slices (or hitting extremely lightly) with the power clubs.

Famed golf writer Pat Ward-Thomas saw O'Connor's style as a 'lovely, rounded movement, strong and yet graceful'. But his Achilles' heel was his occasional susceptibility when putting, principally from short range. But, for all this, O'Connor was a do-or-die player, never afraid to go for broke.

Facing Finsterwald at Lindrick, regardless of a spate of weak putting in the first session, O'Connor was seen by most as being a match for the American, but this encounter was a bitter one. O'Connor started the game well, winning the opening two holes with birdie threes to establish a two-hole lead. O'Connor recalled, 'He was not impressed, and by the steely look in his eye I could see it was going to be a dour struggle, if not quite as fearsome as it transpired.'

The enmity between the players was sparked off by an incident early on. O'Connor found the 3rd green with his approach, getting comfortably by the flagstick in two shots, but his adversary missed the green and chipped up to around six feet. Christy was the first to putt and rolled his ball two feet past the hole. Finsterwald had to hole his for par, but when the ball slid by the hole he reached out and in anger hooked it back with his putter while it was still in motion. O'Connor recalled, 'The crowd encircling the green gasped in astonishment and, before I had time to do or say a thing, the referee moved on to the green and announced, "O'Connor three up."'

Finsterwald, seemingly amazed, exclaimed, 'What did you say? I didn't concede that hole.'

The referee replied, 'Pick up your ball, O'Connor, you're three up.'

After this incident, both men played in stony silence and hardly looked at one another, although O'Connor saw what happened as being nothing to do with anything he had done.

Harry Bradshaw was playing Dick Mayer in the last match of the day right behind O'Connor and Finsterwald. He watched as the American, who was playing his compatriot ahead of his own game, walked to the 4th tee. Bradshaw saw him cracking his driver off the ground and remembered saying to himself, 'Something must have happened.' He later wrote, 'Every Irish doctor in England seemed to be following Christy and myself and some Irish doctors told me what had happened walking to the 4th tee.'

O'Connor concluded the initial 18 holes level with Finsterwald, but O'Connor had made a series of putting errors, and saw himself as having 'tamely surrendered control' and as such was angry with himself.

During the break in the game between O'Connor and Finsterwald, Harry Bradshaw found O'Connor and advised him to knock in every putt, even if it was only two or three inches from the hole. O'Connor made a visit to Jack (brother of Lendrick-born John, who would be the non-playing captain of the European Ryder Cup team in 1979 and 1981) Jacobs's pro shop at Lindrick and purchased a new club. It was unusual for O'Connor to change putters mid-game, but he hadn't felt comfortable and took the risk of switching to a lighter putter.

O'Connor grabbed a quick bowl of soup and spent the remainder of the lunch break on the practice putting green until it was time to resume what was the most high-tension singles he was ever to play.

The gamble seemed to pay off in the afternoon. He was as surprised as anyone else to smack putts down six of the first seven greens at the recommencement of play to open up a six-hole lead after just eight holes.

The weather changed totally from the start of the second round. The wind came up hard. The playing conditions had altered dramatically and Finsterwald just wasn't able to cope. He seemed shattered and his exasperation was made worse as his touch dramatically deserted him as quickly as O'Connor had found his. The American was beside himself as the famed 'luck of the Irish' kicked in, when O'Connor sunk an impudent shot from beneath a bush nestling alongside the 8th green. The situation was almost embarrassing for Finsterwald, as usually the Americans were dynamite on the greens. In his depression, the incident of the morning must have begun to play havoc with and torture his mind.

On the 9th green, the two players had short putts for par. Finsterwald putted first and missed what should have been a tap-in. O'Connor conceded the return putt and Finsterwald strode off the green in a fury towards the 10th hole, leaving O'Connor standing alone on the green. O'Connor recalled that, when he putted, he just missed and, since his ball came to rest no more than an inch from the hole, O'Connor assumed Finsterwald would give it to him for the half and O'Connor picked it up. O'Connor duly stepped forward with the honour to drive off the next tee, but, as he prepared to hit his drive, Finsterwald broke the long silence between the two men. 'Hold it,' he shouted. 'You did not finish out. I'm claiming the hole and it's my honour.'

O'Connor was surprised to lose the hole, and, in his own words, his opponent 'like a drowning man grasping for a lifeline … reintroduced the rule book'.

O'Connor was shocked by the younger man's reaction and didn't like the way he had been goaded into making the error of presuming the putt would be given. But O'Connor didn't lose his focus, although he was incensed by what he saw as unashamed gamesmanship.

Harry Bradshaw said of his countryman after this episode, 'He's the only golfer to my mind who could do that … A good many golfers would have fallen apart after that happened – knowing that the hole was halved and then losing it by this little incident.'

The Irishman won the following hole to recapture his six lead, and Finsterwald didn't win another hole. O'Connor won a categorical seven and six victory with a par on the 12th.

It was reported that both men refused to shake hands after the game but O'Connor, who saw the game as a 'torrid battle', being pockmarked by 'waspish' remarks, had a different memory of events: 'The anger of some of the Americans (and I must add that their officials were outraged by their conduct) was highlighted, too, by the reaction of Dow Finsterwald, after I murdered him. In spite of pleas from players on both teams … my humiliated opponent was so disgruntled he declined to shake my hand.'

Even later, in the clubhouse, when members of both teams attempted to pour oil on troubled waters, Finsterwald was unyielding in his enmity.

O'Connor managed Finsterwald well because he had come up the hard way and had learned to adopt a rock-hard attitude on the greens. He admitted, 'They called me a big, moody boor who would not pass the time of day on the golf course ... Perhaps I was, but I did not mean to look so grim. It was my way of concentrating. Deep down, I was happy at my work.'

O'Connor was to 'cherish' this game amongst his Ryder Cup exploits and agreed with the analysis of the time that saw the encounter as being a 'classic – with a needle'.

O'Connor's performance in a bitterly contested match confirmed that he was blessed with magnificent talent, but he also had a ferocious competitive streak and a ruthless attitude. However, although the game had been aggressive, it had also been a class act.

With Bousfield five up early in the afternoon round against Lionel Hebert, Bernard Hunt five up on Doug Ford with nine to play, and O'Connor winning half-a-dozen of the first eight holes in his encounter with Finsterwald, an upset looked at least possible. As the crowds crisscrossed the Lindrick course, trying to get a better view of events, intermittent cheers would echo over the greens from different parts of the course as yet another home victory was confirmed.

The defeat of the USA was posted on the wooden scoreboards. The headlines of the next day would focus on the rift between Rees and Weetman, but what was grabbing the attention of every British and Irish supporter on the last day of the Ryder Cup at Lindrick was the prospect of a rare victory for their team.

HOLE BY HOLE – MATCH SEVEN																				
Players	1	2	3	4	5	6	7	8	9	Out	10	11	12	13	14	15	16	17	18	In
Finsterwald	5	4	4	4	4	3	4	5	4	37	4	3	4	3	4	4	5	5	3	35 72
O'Connor	4	3	3	4	5	3	5	3	4	34	4	3	5	4	5	4	5	4	3	37 71
Finsterwald	5	4	4	5	5	3	5	4	4	39	5	3	4							Won 7 & 6
O'Connor	4	4	3	4	4	3	4	3	X	-	4	2	4							

CHAPTER SEVENTEEN

It's Really Something When Bradshaw Doesn't Make a Putt

DICK MAYER (USA)

V

HARRY BRADSHAW (GREAT BRITAIN AND IRELAND)

1957 was Dick Mayer's golden year. In June, the golfer from St Petersburg, Florida, finished the regulation 72 holes of the US Open at the Inverness Club, at Toledo, Ohio, tied with defending champion Cary Middlecoff of Memphis, Tennessee. Dick won the 18-hole play-off 72 to 79 and took his winner's purse of $7,200. In Chicago, during August, he won $50,000 (courtesy of George May, golf's 'King of Promotion') at the Tam O'Shanter World Championship of Golf. His income was at least doubled by way of exhibitions and promotions that came with his growing fame. Mayer topped the PGA Tour money list by a long way with winnings of $65,835 and won the PGA Player of the Year Award.

When Christy O'Connor learned that his fellow Irishman Harry Bradshaw was playing Dick Mayer, the reigning US Open Champion, in the singles, he responded by putting his hands to his face and saying, 'Oh, Brad, I feel sorry for you. He's after beating myself and Eric.'

Harry replied, 'I'll knock in putt for putt with him.'

Harry would not be far off the mark in his prophecy.

Harry Bradshaw was born on 9 October 1913 in the village of Killincarrig, Co. Wicklow, around a mile from Delgany Golf Club. Harry's father Ned was the professional at Delgany. After a few years, the Bradshaws moved to a house close to the course where Harry, the oldest of six children, swiftly fell in love with the game.

The original Irish name of the area which is now County Wicklow was *Contae Chill Mhantáin* meaning 'Mantan's Church'; 'Wicklow' comes from the Old Norse *Wykinglo* (Vikings' Meadow). That particular part of the Irish Republic lies on the east coast of Ireland, immediately south of Dublin.

Wicklow is often known as 'The Garden of Ireland', and is regarded as an exceptionally beautiful place, with its many gently sloping hills and lakes. The area has also been called 'the last county' as it was the last of the original counties to be established in 1606 from land previously part of County Dublin.

A 'military road', stretching from Rathfarnham to Aughavannagh, cuts through the mountains. It was built by the British Army to assist them in crushing rebels still active in the Wicklow Mountains after the failed 1798 rebellion, providing them swift entry to an area that had been a hotbed of Irish rebellion for centuries. Several barracks to house the soldiers were built along the route. As such, the place of

Harry's origins was intensely Irish in many ways and something culturally quite apart from the backgrounds and influences of most of his team-mates.

Like Fred Daly, Harry's fellow Irishman and friend of later years, Harry's involvement with golf began with caddying before he became an assistant to his father at Delgany. It was obvious in those initial years that Harry had a talent for the game, and the advantage of growing up on a course allowed him to work on his technique and develop as a player. He practised hard and built a method and style that was to serve him well.

From boyhood, Harry developed his own decidedly individual, rounded, three-quarter swing. While anything but elegant (certainly not textbook), it encompassed a loop as well as a prominent sway; but it was intuitive, uninhibited and carried out with a beautiful rhythm. Bernard Darwin, golf writer with *The Times*, described Harry's action as 'rugged and rustic'. According to Harry's biographer, golf journalist Dermot Gilleece, as far as golfing technique was concerned, 'Harry was at all times a pragmatist.'

Harry also had an odd grip, with three fingers of his right hand overlapping his left. For all this, he was a splendidly reliable player who consistently kept his ball in play. Harry had an outstanding touch on and around the greens; his chipping was magnificent and he hit his putts with a positive smack. He kept his head down until he heard the ball clatter into the cup. From an early age, Harry was always reasonably good at the game, though he could never have been considered long, even when he used the orthodox Vardon grip. Putting was his weak spot until he underwent a period of training from the toughest taskmaster any young professional could have had. Father Gleeson was a curate in Bray and, when Harry met the priest going about his business, Gleeson would ask the youngster how he had been playing.

Almost invariably, Harry would have to report that he did very well except for his putting. The priest told him, 'I'll have to take you in hand.'

Harry later claimed that he would have been terrified out of the game if he knew what this resolution meant for him. 'Now,' Gleeson would say as he and Harry went out to play at Delgany, 'whenever you get the ball on the green, you must hole it in one stroke.'

Harry recollected that sometimes it took close to four hours to play nine holes, with Father Gleeson adamant that they shouldn't move on to the next hole before Harry holed out. The curate would sit on his golf bag at the side of the green, while Harry repeatedly putted from the same spot. The same procedure was carried out on numerous evenings when Father Gleeson had time to spare, until the pupil began to dread the sight of the man.

But, slowly, Harry understood that the way to get around in a reasonable time was to hit his approach shots closer to the hole. As a result, he focused on getting up and down from 100 yards and in the process developed a short game that would be envied wherever he went.

Harry was 40 when he made his relatively late Ryder Cup debut in 1953, but he was selected for Great Britain and Ireland again in 1955 and once more in 1957. He was the first golfer from the Irish Republic to play in the Ryder Cup and won two, lost two and halved one of his five matches in the tournament. The part he played in the Ryder Cup was always to be something that Harry treasured. As many players struggled to maintain their game with the onset of middle age, Harry appeared to get better as he got older and his greatest triumphs came late in his career.

In the edgy match at Wentworth in 1953, he won both his matches. His foursomes victory over Walter Burkemo and Cary Middlecoff was a very close-run thing. Fred Daly, Harry's partner that day, had to hole a putt of about four feet on the final green to win the match. In his singles, Harry beat Fred Haas, but Great Britain and Ireland lost by one point.

In the 1940s and 50s, Harry dominated in the Irish Professional Championship: he won it on 10 occasions between 1941 and 1957. He was victorious in the Irish Open at Royal Portrush in 1947, fending off Fred Daly, amongst others.

Daly had won the Open Championship at Royal Liverpool, where he and Harry had travelled and stayed in the same guest house throughout the Open. Daly's victory in the Open was a breakthrough for Irish golf and it was thought that it would be the start of a green wave of success. Harry began to be seen as a successor to Fred. But Daly had come to Portrush looking to achieve a unique double. However, he was to be denied as Harry's four rounds of 73, 74, 73 and 70 gave him victory by two shots over Belgian Flory van Donck. Harry repeated that feat in 1949.

It was some years before Harry won a tournament in Britain. He came close to triumph at the Open

Championship at Royal St George's, Sandwich, in 1949, but during the second round he was robbed by a peculiar episode at the 5th hole.

Harry arrived in Sandwich in top form and was optimistic after leading the qualifying with rounds of 67 and 72, pulling away from big names like Bobby Locke and Max Faulkner. He carried on playing well in the opening round on Wednesday, concluding with a 68 which left him one off the pace.

Harry began his second round pretty well until he came to the 5th, a long par 4 of 420 yards. He struck his tee-shot and watched as the strong breeze took it towards the light rough. Harry was unconcerned, but, as he approached the ball, he was astonished to find it sitting in a broken beer bottle.

'The Brad' (as many fellow players and fans knew Harry) was uncertain of how the rules applied (at that time, he would not have been awarded a free drop). His playing partner was as clueless as he was. Could he drop it out? Would he be penalised? He waited for a quarter of an hour hoping that an answer might be provided, but there were no officials to be found and in an era without mobile phones or walkie-talkies, rather than wait any longer for a ruling, quicksilver Harry decided to play the ball as it lay. He grabbed his 9-iron and, with his eyes tightly closed, turning his head away, he whacked into the bottle which shattered into pieces. However, the ball only travelled around 20 yards and he took a double bogey at the hole. Harry finished with a six, but his bad fortune didn't perturb him. He went on to score a round of 77. It says much for the Irishman that he was able to put the experience behind him and in the two final rounds managed 68 and 70 to lead in the clubhouse with a total of 283.

Locke was Harry's closest challenger. The South African produced a masterful birdie at the 17th and this was followed with a par on the 18th to set up a 36-hole play-off. Regrettably, the play-off was an anticlimax. Harry seemed to lose focus and motivation as Locke fixed his eyes on the prize, producing rounds of 67 and 68 to defeat Harry by a dozen shots. The beer bottle might well have stopped Harry lifting the famous claret jug.

It was a huge disappointment for Harry, made worse when he was told that he would not be considered for the Ryder Cup which would be played at Ganton later that year. His status within the PGA as an 'overseas player' disallowed his selection. It would be four more years before he was to make his Ryder Cup debut at Wentworth as a member of the first Great Britain and Ireland team with Fred Daly under the captaincy of Henry Cotton.

Prior to the 1953 Cup, Cotton devised a plan to create a strong team spirit. The players practised and roomed together, while there were regular discussions about tactics.

When choosing the foursomes pairings for Day One, Cotton decided that the two Irishmen should be partners. Both Daly and Bradshaw were happy about the decision. They had played together on a regular basis and knew each other well.

As the more experienced player, Daly led the way and the Irishmen had an encouraging start against the Americans Cary

Middlecoff and Walter Burkemo. Fred and Harry concluded the morning three holes in front. Following lunch, Middlecoff and Burkemo pulled back; however, with nine holes to go, Bradshaw and Daly had reclaimed their three-hole advantage.

But, with the clubhouse in sight, the Irishmen wavered after some magnificent play from Burkemo. With only the 18th left to play, the lead was down to one. At the 18th, Harry hit a bad drive into the left semi-rough and then Fred hit a wood right up to near the green. Harry was left with a shot of close to 70 yards. He walked up to have a look. By his own admission, 'his knees were knocking' as he considered his options. There were 25,000 people there; some of them were hanging out of the trees. He had never played in front of a crowd like that in all his life.

Harry came back and told Fred that he didn't know whether to play a nine or a ten. His partner told him to play what he liked. This advice gave Harry confidence. He understood that it doesn't matter what club you hit. Fred, unlike many people, had not told his friend, 'Leave it close and I'll hole the putt.'

So Harry knocked it in to six feet and Fred holed it while their opponents missed their chance for three. There was a mad rush for Fred and Harry. He was to reflect later that, if it hadn't been for the presence of the police, Fred would have been knocked into the hole after the ball; Harry and Fred were never beaten as a pair.

However, the Irish victory was to be the only euphoric moment in a disappointing day. Cotton's team were 3–1 down and the great man let it be known he was looking to 'kick their backsides'.

On the second day, chastised by their captain, Great Britain and Ireland came out fighting in the singles and the Irishmen once more led the attack.

First off was Dai Rees, but he lost to Jack Burke, but, behind him, Fred Daly simply smashed Ted Kroll nine and seven. Wins for Harry Weetman and Eric Brown pulled the teams level with four matches out on the course. Bradshaw, brimming with self-assurance following his foursomes triumph, had the anchor role, confronting Fred Haas, who had been left out on the first day by US captain Lloyd Mangrum. Harry was one up at lunch and extended his lead in the afternoon to record his second Ryder Cup victory, three and two.

Sadly, the Irish heroism did not bring an overall victory for Great Britain and Ireland, as the inexperienced Peter Alliss and Bernard Hunt collapsed under American firepower and the USA once more retained the Cup by just one point.

In Harry's biography *The Brad*, he recalls his first tournament, the 1933 Adgey Cup, which was presented by the Northern Ireland Bromford agent of the same name. It was a 36-hole stroke-play event. Harry was leading the field by two, with three holes to play only to throw this away as he became overawed by the size of the gallery. Willie Nolan, the Portmarnock professional, won the event.

Harry won the Bromford-Adgey Cup in 1938 but remained at Delgany until 1941. Then he became the professional at Kilcroney Golf and Country Club near Bray. At that point, he was competing regularly in professional tournaments and was one of Ireland's brightest talents.

Moving to Kilcroney proved to be successful on a number

of levels for Harry as it was there he met his wife Elizabeth. They married and started a family during the War years. After his near-miss at Sandwich, in 1950, Harry had moved from Kilcroney to the professional's post at Portmarnock and in 1952 broke his duck in Britain by winning the inaugural Dunbar Open in Scotland.

Harry dealt with matters in a swift and efficient manner. Henry Longhurst observed, 'He can size up a shot, choose his club, hit the ball on to the green and be walking after it, all in the time that it takes an American to test the direction of the wind.'

By 1953, Harry had firmly established himself as one of the leading players on tour. He won the British Masters that year, a feat he achieved again two years later.

At the Thunderbird Ranch, during the Ryder Cup of 1955, many of the Great Britain and Ireland team tasted desert-style golf for the first time and they all struggled in conditions that were strange and uncomfortable for them. It was difficult to acclimatise to the Bermuda grass which was inclined to clutch the ball.

Skipper Rees, while missing an Irishman in Fred Daly, had been supplied with another, Christy O'Connor; however, he was left out of the opening-day foursomes, in which Harry and Rees met Sam Snead and Cary Middlecoff, the best American pairing.

Snead and Middlecoff started powerfully, dominating the early holes, but, little by little, the Celtic duo pegged back their illustrious foe and by lunch things were level. Bradshaw and Rees snatched the lead by taking the 1st hole after the break, but, although they recorded 10 threes in the course of the match, the Americans won three and two.

It was to be another disappointing opening day for Great Britain and Ireland with John Fallen and John Jacobs getting the only win of the day. Rees put his finger on the major factor holding his players back: the quality of their putting. He said, 'It's really something when Bradshaw doesn't make a putt.'

Harry had a titanic war with Jack Burke in the singles. In the morning round, despite a poor opening nine holes, Harry played half a dozen consecutive threes and made 31 to go into lunch all square. In the afternoon, it was still hard to separate them, and both men seemed to be giving as good as they were getting. But Burke eventually edged in front, establishing a three-hole lead which he maintained on his way to a three and two victory. After the game, according to the referee, Harry did not make one poor shot, which says much for Jack Burke's performance.

In his 1957 singles match with Dick Mayer, Harry's prediction that he would 'knock in putt for putt' with Mayer started promisingly, when he won the first three holes, including holing a bunker shot at the 3rd, which brought thunderous applause from the gallery. Harry recalled, when walking to the 4th tee, Mayer telling him, 'You're a great trap player, Harry.'

'Yes,' Harry replied. 'I hole four or five in a round as a rule.'

Mayer told his opponent that he hoped he wouldn't do that on that particular morning.

According to Harry, this was 'giving him the old one and

two': flattery followed by what was effectively a wish for the Irishman to have bad luck.

By lunch, Mayer was one hole in front.

Harry pulled level by winning the opening hole of the second 18, curiously off a bogey five, and from then on there wasn't more than a hole in it.

While Harry's 1957 battle with Mayer continued, the rest of the Great Britain and Ireland team were inflicting a series of heavy defeats on their opponents. Halfway through the afternoon, Harry knew the Cup had been won and lost. But the Irishman had something to play for; it was his third and final crack at the Americans; he was 44 years old and had been starved of success since his Dunlop Masters victory in 1955.

After once more dropping behind, Harry won the 14th to equal the score. Four holes were shared coming to the last, Harry got down in two from well short of the last green to score a half and finish the only game of the entire event that made the 36th hole.

The game was played in front of massive crowds that included the young Jimmy Patiño, tin magnate and future owner of Valderrama, in Spain, venue of the 1997 Ryder Cup. The Ryder Cup of 1957 was his first.

Patiño was something of a playboy during the mid-1950s and he knew the likes of Peter Alliss and Dai Rees. He'd been to Italy for the Italian Open. In those days, the players didn't have their own caddies, and Rees hired an Italian caddie, but the man was unable to speak a word of English. The Welshman couldn't make the relationship work and eventually took his bag away from the local carrier. Patiño asked Rees if he wanted him to carry his bags. Rees had no idea what to pay the millionaire, but Jimmy was willing to do the job for free. However, as a mark of his appreciation, Rees gave him two tickets to the Ryder Cup at Lindrick. Patiño loved the event, seeing it as a great way of bringing people together and was pleased his friends were successful.

When Patiño took charge of Valderrama, he launched his personal crusade to bring the Ryder Cup to Spain. The Bolivian billionaire understood that the Ryder Cup at Valderrama would act as a catalyst as the golf coast reasserted itself as Europe's finest golf destination.

Observer journalist Pat Ward Thomas described the victory scene at Lindrick in 1957:

> Suddenly, before anyone could believe it, the deed was done, the Americans had been put to flight as never before ... Last of all Bradshaw brought a wonderful even match with Mayer to its fitting end by getting down in two from well short of the last green. An unforgettable day was done.

But, ever the perfectionist, Harry felt he should really have got the full point having three-putted the 9th green twice. He saw this as being the reason for his failure to conclude his Ryder Cup career with a win.

After the match, it became known that Harry owed a debt to massage, and the skills of one practitioner of the art in

179

particular. Prior to the match, *Golf Illustrated* (3 October 1957) had told the public,

> During the actual match any members of either side who want a massage will find Mr. W. Glover, who has been provided by Castle Equipment, in co-operation with Harry Weetman, at the clubhouse with all the latest masseur's equipment.

It seems the estimable Glover had treated a number of players on both sides and was said to have managed to deal with Bradshaw's back in a 'most satisfactory manner'.

Suddenly, before anyone could take it in, the Americans had been defeated and it was hard to know quite how to respond.

HOLE BY HOLE – MATCH EIGHT																			
Players	1	2	3	4	5	6	7	8	9	Out	10	11	12	13	14	15	16	17	18	All Square
Mayer	5	5	3	4	5	3	4	3	4	36	5	3	4	4	5	4	5	3	3	36 72
Bradshaw	4	4	2	5	4	3	5	3	5	35	5	3	4	5	4	5	5	5	3	39 74
Mayer	6	4	3	5	3	3	4	4	4	36	5	3	3	4	5	4	5	4	3	36 72
Bradshaw	4	4	3	5	3	3	4	4	5	36	4	3	4	4	4	4	5	4	3	35 71

Day two result: USA 1½, Great Britain and Ireland 6½
Overall match score: USA 4½, Great Britain and Ireland 7½

CHAPTER EIGHTEEN

Pride of the Isles

After 1957, Dai Rees's men had diverse and interesting lives. What follows gives a brief description of what the future held for the 'Victors of Lindrick'.

Bernard Hunt, 27-year-old Hartsbourne assistant, had his first professional success in 1953 when he won the Assistants' Championship. That same year he won the Spalding Tournament, a success he repeated this year. He also finished third in this season's Dunlop Tournament. A member of the 1953 Ryder Cup team, Hunt's other successes included wins in the 1953 Gleneagles-Saxone Tournament.

Golf Illustrated – 3 October 1957

The best season of Bernard's regular career in terms of prize money was 1963, when he won £7,209. In that year, he became the first player to win four £1,000 titles in a season. But, by the introduction of the formal European Tour in 1972, Bernard was past his peak; however, he finished in the top 20 on the money list in 1973.

Bernard played on the European Seniors Tour in four of its first seven seasons (1992 to 1998) but his opportunity to make an impact at this level was limited, as he was 62 at the time the Tour was founded. Hunt's best season as a Senior was 1994, when he came 15th on the Order of Merit, having earned £15,361, but, in an Indian summer of a competitive career, he acquitted himself well overall.

Year	Tour	Order of Merit Winnings	Ranking Position
1998	Seniors Tour	£7,178	61
1997	Seniors Tour	£5,561	69
1996	Seniors Tour	£5,791	49
1995	Seniors Tour	£6,836	36
1994	Seniors Tour	£15,361	15
1993	Seniors Tour	£7,893	29
1992	Seniors Tour	£2,947	41
1977	European Tour	£1,420	222
1975	European Tour	£1,443	87
1974	European Tour	£3,274	42
1973	European Tour	£4,876	17
1972	European Tour	£2,933	23
1971	European Tour	£3,864	14

In 1961, the Ryder Cup format changed from 36-hole to 18-hole matches, and, in 1963 and 1965, Bernard was sent out in every series, a dozen matches. This was at a time when the USA were masters of the Ryder Cup and Bernard's record of four wins and two halved matches out of 12 is worthy of credit. His partnership with Neil Coles started in 1963 and they played eight matches together. Bernard remembered that there were always individuals on both sides who were frantic for victory. For Bernard, Brian Huggett was like that. If two of these desperadoes meet in competition, it can be the recipe for a great game. Bernard was partnering Neil Coles against Julian Boros and Tony Lema. Lema is quoted as saying to Bernard, 'If you couldn't putt, you would never get round.'

Coles and Hunt won on the 18th.

In his last appearance in the Ryder Cup, in 1969 at Royal Birkdale, Bernard finished positively. With Peter Butler, he lost by one hole in the foursomes to Jack Nicklaus and Dan Sikes, but, alongside Maurice Bembridge, he managed to wrestle a half from Tommy Aaron and Ray Floyd so forcing a 16–16 tie. Looking back, he thought his side should have won that encounter. He recalled how he and Bembridge were level going down the 18th. Maurice and Bernard were both on the green in two. The Americans got their four and so Hunt and Bembridge needed birdie putts for the win. Maurice was closer and so Hunt went first. They both missed and the match was halved. Afterwards, the Great Britain and Ireland captain that year Eric Brown, in Bernard's words, gave him 'a bollocking'. Brown maintained that, as Bernard was the better putter, he should have let Bembridge go first and get the half so that Bernard could have made a focused attempt at the three.

After taking on the role as non-playing captain of the team at Muirfield in 1973, Bernard thought the 19–13 result would have been much closer if Bernard Gallacher had not fallen sick following the first day's play. Bernard knew that this, added to Christy O'Connor's reticence to play a second singles on the final day, would mean even less chance of his side doing as well as it might. However, following a few glasses of red wine at lunchtime, the Irishman had agreed to take on the great Tom Weiskopf, who had won the Open Championship at Troon earlier that year. O'Connor halved the game, but Bernard confessed that he had told a sceptical Weiskopf that, after a couple of glasses of 'the red infuriator', O'Connor was unbeatable.

Bernard's long-term battle with America concluded in 1975 when he was once more non-playing skipper at Laurel Valley, in Pennsylvania. Arnold Palmer was the American captain, a man and a player that Bernard saw as a great personality and with whom he always got on very well.

Such a protracted competitive relationship is bound to incite all sorts of feelings, especially given the domination of the USA over Bernard's tenure, but there were a number of Americans that Bernard both liked and respected, and a couple of names particularly stood out. He liked Ted Kroll as a man and admired his New York relaxed manner. Bernard also had a high opinion of Kroll's swing, likening his style to that of Mark O'Meara, in that Kroll's swing was relatively short, but he consistently hit the ball with power.

TOURNAMENTS AND AWARDS

1952 Coombe Hill Assistants

1953 Coombe Hill Assistants, Saxone/Gleneagles Hotel
    Goodwin Foursomes (with Jack Hargreaves)

1954 Goodwin Foursomes (with WS Collins)

1956 Egyptian Open

1958 Palace Hotel Torquay

1960 Pickering Cup (with GM Hunt)

1961 German Open

1962 Brazilian Open

1963 British Masters, Smart Weston

1965 British Masters

1967 French Open

1970 Agfacolor Film, Sumrie Clothes Better-Ball
    (with Neil Coles)

1971 WD and HO Wills

1973 Sumrie Clothes Better-Ball (with Neil Coles)

TEAM APPEARANCES

Ryder Cup (representing Great Britain): 1953, 1957,
    1959, 1961, 1963, 1965, 1967, 1969

World Cup of Golf (representing England): 1958, 1959,
    1960, 1962, 1963, 1964, 1968

Double Diamond: 1971, 1972, 1973

Open: 3rd= 1960, 4th 1964, 5th= 1955, 1965, 11th 1959,
    1963, 16th= 1962, 20th= 1971

Bernard Hunt has never ceased to study golf and he has journeyed tens of thousands of miles during his time as a player to better his game and his income. At the start of the 1960s, he was a habitual visitor to the American circuit during the first part of the year; he would then contest the British tournaments and wind up in South America at the end of the year. Although he did not win an event in the USA, he was victorious in the Egyptian Open in 1956 and the Brazilian Open in 1962.

Living in Woking, Surrey, Bernard became the first head professional at Foxhills (which now has a course named after him – The Bernard Hunt Course) and where he served for 25 years. He made himself a force in Pro-Am and Senior tournaments. Now, an MBE, with a build not much different from his heyday (6ft 2in, 14st 10lb) and an interest in gardening, Bernard is captain of the Professional Golfers' Association of England and he continues to enjoy teaching and his life in the game. To this day, his swing is still solid.

Christy O'Connor, from Bundoran, has only shown his best form late this season. But it won him the Match-Play Championship. Last year he tied for the Spalding Tournament and in the previous year won the Swallow Penfold Tournament. He played in the last Ryder Cup match.

Golf Illustrated – 3 October 1957

Christy won almost all that British professional golf had to offer and, at his best in the 1960s, he was one of the top players in Europe.

At the Eldorado Club, Palm Springs, in 1959, O'Connor was defeated by Art Wall in the Ryder Cup singles. In the foursomes, he was paired with Peter Alliss. This was the start of a long partnership between the two men. Up against Art Wall and Doug Ford, they combined well and won three and two, the visitors' only foursomes victory of the day.

The Great Britain and Ireland team had been involved in a horrifying flight from Los Angeles to Palm Springs. High above the San Jacinto Mountains, their plane flew into a vicious storm and fell 4,000 feet before the pilot could regain control and turn back to Los Angeles.

According to O'Connor, it was the most terrifying experience of his life. After landing back at Los Angeles, the entire team made for the nearest bar and downed copious amounts of brandy. Belfast-based Norman Drew was one of those drinkers and he later started the 'Long Drop Club' to celebrate the shared escape. Club members agreed to toast the founder members at 5.30 p.m. on 29 October every year.

The terrifying experience did much to bring the team together but the US took back the Ryder Cup, inflicting a heavy defeat on the visitors.

O'Connor and Alliss were to play a dozen matches as a pair between 1959 and 1969, winning five, losing six and halving one. Their characters were quite unalike, they were not particularly friendly, although they got on very well together on the golf course, and came from completely different backgrounds, but they made an outstanding team. According to Alliss, they were both suspect on short putts and, as such, were cautious not to leave each other awkward-length putts, a fine example of knowing one another's weaknesses as well as strengths. O'Connor did have a swift, somewhat snatchy style, but he regarded overdoing practice shots as being his prime flaw, he claimed this made him feel too loose and relaxed and he played the worse for it.

Alliss rated Christy as a 'wonderful partner', seeing the Irishman as brave, and having 'a wonderful aura about him'. In the first match they played as a pair, in the 1959 Ryder Cup, on one of the early holes, Alliss hit the ball into the bushes and apologised to his partner. O'Connor turned to Alliss and said, 'Listen, I know you're trying to do the very best you can, so, if we're going to play well together, we don't want any more apologising.'

And that's how the pair played from then on; with an ethos of professional trust. They would encourage each other. But the Bundoran boy played the most magnificent shots. At times, Alliss thought he had lost it; downhill, wind left to right, out of bounds on the right, small green. But they would usually come out of it one or two up with just a couple to play. Having no fear, O'Connor would say, 'They're in trouble. I think I'll just cut a driver in there.'

Alliss always did his best for O'Connor and he got the same in return. Alliss had the most amazing confidence in him. They holed putts when it mattered and became a very solid partnership. Over the years O'Connor and Alliss had the ability to surprise the best that America could throw at them.

In 1958, O'Connor left Bundoran for Killarney. This was swiftly followed in April 1959 by another move to Royal Dublin. Years later, he reflected, 'Tactically, it was the best decision I ever made.' He was able to play all year round on the championship links course and, crucially, with his increasingly demanding travel commitments, it was close to an international airport.

At the end of the 1950s, O'Connor experienced a protracted sequence of important victories, including the Swallow-Penfold, the Dunlop Masters in 1956 and 1959, the PGA Match Play Championship, the Daks and the Martini tournaments. He had a propensity to push through a bunch of players and grab wins with a low final round. In the 1956 Masters, he made up half-a-dozen on Eric Brown, having a final round of 67 in a troublingly high wind at Prestwick. In 1959, in the same event at Portmarnock, O'Connor rescued the professionals from potential embarrassment by overhauling the amateur Joe Carr with a final round of 66.

The one outstanding disappointment in O'Connor's career is his failure to win the Open Championship, although he tried 26 times from 1951 to 1979. For all this, he had one of the best and most consistent records in the event of any of the British professionals of his era. He invariably rose to the occasion in that tournament. At Lytham in 1958, he was leading, following opening rounds of 67 and 68; that 135 aggregate was the lowest since Henry Cotton's 134 at Sandwich in 1934. But O'Connor was playing behind Peter Thomson and Dave Thomas in the final two rounds. Thirty-six holes were then played on the last day; O'Connor was constantly held up by Thomson and has always felt cheated, as he considered that the Australian deliberately played slowly to unsettle him. O'Connor appealed to the official Royal and

Ancient match referee and directly to Thomson at the lunch break, but his protests fell on deaf ears. He dropped back in the third round, as he lost concentration, falling away to a 73, which left him three off the lead that was held by Thomson. But, although still delayed, O'Connor managed to concentrate better in the afternoon and recovered, coming to the last hole with his partner Argentinean Leopoldo Ruiz with a chance of outright victory. Christy needed a par 4 to force a play-off with Thomson and Thomas who were already in the clubhouse. But he reckoned that, if he could make a birdie three at the 72nd hole, he would win the Championship.

At Lytham, the 18th was 379 yards. O'Connor made the decision to assault it with a drive and a wedge. There was a hold-up, although not Thomson's doing on this occasion, as the marshals had been unable to stop the gallery from encroaching on to the 18th fairway. The crowd control was so poor that the final pair had only half the fairway at which to shoot. Impatient with the waiting, O'Connor aimed at the bunkers along the left, but played short with a 3-wood.

O'Connor and his partner bunkered their tee-shots. Ruiz took two to get out and his challenge ended. Christy needed five shots: a par 4 would have put him in the play-off place with Thomson and fellow Aussie Dave Thomas. But he splashed out, pitched too strongly and his putt to make the play-off finished on the lip of the hole.

Thomson won the play-off with some ease by four shots. O'Connor finished third with Eric Brown. He commented afterwards, 'The reality is that I lost that Open not on the last hole but before that and I blame Peter Thomson.'

In 1959, O'Connor finished in fifth place and in 1961 he was once more joint third. In the 1965 Open, he managed equal second, two shots behind Peter Thompson (five-times winner of the title). O'Connor's record in the Open during the 20 years from 1955 was more consistent than any player in Britain or Ireland; between 1958 and 1969, he finished in the top six on seven occasions; 10 times he finished in the top 10, and was in the top 20 on 15 occasions.

The Ryder Cups of the 1960s were a mixture of success and failure for O'Connor, playing for a Great Britain and Ireland team that seemed destined to be the perennial underdogs. At Lytham in 1961 and at East Lake, Atlanta, in 1963, O'Connor made just two and a half points from nine games. However, in 1965 at Royal Birkdale, O'Connor and Peter Alliss fought like tigers to win three of their four games as a pair.

They played some magnificent golf in the foursomes on the opening afternoon, beating Billy Casper and Gene Littler. But the following morning they got slaughtered in the fourballs by Arnold Palmer and Dave Marr. That was a very extraordinary occurrence for Alliss and O'Connor and, by way of proving it, they went on to beat the same pair on the 18th in the afternoon.

But in 1967 in Houston they were defeated in their three games together. O'Connor lost his singles to Bobby Nichols. However, he played a crucial role in the extraordinary tied fixture at Royal Birkdale in 1969, winning two points out of four, despite a troublesome back. Paired for the last time with Peter Alliss, O'Connor halved a foursomes match with Billy Casper and Frank Beard. O'Connor was 45 years old, but continued to be the star of the Great Britain and Ireland team, winning three of his four matches at Birkdale in 1969.

Christy seemed to win the big-money events: for instance, in the Alcan tournament in 1968 and the John Player Classic of 1970 he claimed first prize of £25,000, he seemed not in the least disconcerted at being hounded by Tony Jacklin, the US Open Champion at that time.

At Old Warson, St Louis, in 1971, Neil Coles was partnering O'Connor in the opening fourballs and asked the Irishman who should make the opening drive. After a number of efforts to get a decision, the pair got to the 1st tee with the question unresolved. Their rivals on that day, Billy Casper and Miller Barber, were shocked to see them toss a coin. However, having trusted to fate, it was kind to them, and they won the match.

In 1973, O'Connor played in his last Ryder Cup. During practice, he made an incredible round of 61. He covered the back nine in 29 shots. He later said that it was the right score on the wrong day! Christy was to play five matches in total at Muirfield for a return of one and half points. Such was captain Bernard Hunt's faith in O'Connor that, after two days with the score at 8–8, he played him in both the morning and afternoon singles on the final day. O'Connor later said, 'I reckon I did as much as I could to vindicate his confidence in me.'

Yet again, alongside Coles (whom he partnered on three occasions), he was victorious in their opening foursomes, defeating Tom Weiskopf and Jesse Snead. O'Connor was beaten in his next three games. Although shooting 71 in his singles match against Snead, the best round by the home side, he lost by one hole.

O'Connor told his skipper that he was too tired to play after lunch. As such, he downed some quantity of red wine with his meal. However, Hunt, seeing that the USA required just three points from the eight afternoon games to win the Cup, looked to O'Connor to pick up his clubs. The captain calculated that a 'fuelled' O'Connor would be a match for any adversary. Topped up by the odd slug from hip-flasks carried by his supporters, O'Connor faced the US Open Champion Tom Weiskopf.

O'Connor was one down with four to play, but won the 15th to pull level. He then got up and down from a greenside bunker to halve the match. It was a characteristically indomitable display from the Irishman and a good finale to his career in the Ryder Cup, of which he said, 'They were great times and I have some magnificent memories.'

His single disappointment was never to be invited to captain a Ryder Cup team: 'I would have loved it. With my experience, I might have been able to do the job better than others, maybe, but only with full control.'

O'Connor has conceded that his Ryder Cup statistics are not exceptional; 13 points from 36 matches is a modest total in the scheme of things. But, looking back, he commented, 'Things have changed so much since I played in the Ryder Cup. When we took on the Americans, we were still club professionals while they were full-time tournament players …We were still teaching, trying to make a few bucks to support our families. It was difficult and it was very hard work. When I was in

Bundoran, I used to give lessons in the summer from 8.30 in the morning until dark, and then I went back to the shop and spent another couple of hours fixing clubs.'

Being amongst Europe's top professionals, O'Connor played more than some of his team-mates and was frequently matched with the best the USA could offer. In *Himself* by Seamus Smith, O'Connor told of how, 'Every team had passengers ... There were those who got sick, scared to death of the big occasions, and that added extra pressure on the top four or five players who had to play every match – and win!'

O'Connor seemed to be inspired when playing in his own country and won many titles in Ireland during his long career. He represented his nation in the Canada Cup 15 times between 1956 and 1975. In the heat and the thin atmosphere of Mexico City in 1958, with Harry Bradshaw, Christy won the team event.

Followed by the so-called 'Black Pack' (the many priests to be found in the O'Connor gallery), he won five Carroll's tournaments. Nearly 40 years on, O'Connor's eagle, birdie, eagle finish, provoking the local crowd into wild jubilation, to win the Carroll's Irish Championship at the Royal Dublin Golf Club in 1966, still ranks as the finest finish to any Irish professional golf tournament and is a special memory for anyone who was there.

O'Connor won the Gallagher event three times, all against the regular tournament field, and, from 1958, when he first won the Irish Professional Championship, Christy was considered the man to beat in that competition.

O'Connor's home town of Galway recognised his achievements in 1970 when they made him their first

Freeman, and, in 1988, the members of the Royal Dublin Club conferred Honorary Life Membership on him.

He won the British PGA Seniors title six times in eight years from 1976, and has also been six-times European Senior Champion and twice World Seniors Champion (in 1976 and 1977). His fine swing lasted over time (the fluidity of his movement had a lot to do with this longevity), serving as the professional at Royal Dublin, having joined that club in 1959.

O'Connor triumphed 25 times in European PGA tournaments and won 10 Irish Championships (a record he shares with his late great friend Harry Bradshaw), his last at the age of 51, producing a catalogue of phenomenal shots in the process. He never made a concerted effort on the US circuit and he never played in the Masters, although he was invited to do so on several occasions; one of his regrets is that he failed to take up this challenge. That he might have done well was confirmed by Billy Casper, a Ryder Cup opponent, who also met O'Connor many times at tournament level. Casper told him, 'It's a good thing you weren't born in the United States, otherwise nobody would have heard of me, or those other two plumbers, Palmer and Nicklaus.'

His nephew and namesake, Christy O'Connor Junior, continued the golfing dynasty after Christy Senior bowed out of the top flight of the game, but he remains arguably the most talented and influential figure ever to come out of the Irish game.

Darren Clarke has defeated the best and fellow Ulsterman Fred Daly remains the only Irishman to have won the British Open. However, taken overall, Christy O'Connor Senior is the finest of a great bunch. Beyond golf, he is one of Ireland's most famous and well-loved international sports stars – the first Irish sportsman to register on the world stage. Popularly known as simply 'Himself', he is a living legend who continues to roam around tough courses in level par.

TOURNAMENTS AND AWARDS
1956 Dunlop Masters
1957 British Match Play Champion
1958 Irish Professional Champion
1959 Dunlop Masters Daks Tournament
1960 Irish Professional Champion, Ballantine Tournament, Irish Hospitals Tournament
1961 Irish Professional Champion, Irish Hospitals Tournament, Harry Vardon Trophy
1962 Irish Professional Champion, Irish Hospitals Tournament, Harry Vardon Trophy
1963 Irish Professional Champion, Martini Tournament, Carroll's Sweet Afton
1964 Martini Tournament, Carroll's Sweet Afton
1965 Irish Professional Champion
1966 Irish Professional Champion, Carroll's Sweet Afton, Gallagher Ulster
1967 Carroll's Sweet Afton
1968 Carroll's No 1 Tournament, Gallagher Ulster Alcan International
1969 Gallagher Ulster Irish Southern PGA
1970 John Player Classic

Eric Brown, 32, from Buchanan Castle, has played in the last two Ryder Cup matches. He won the Masters' Tournament after being third in the Spalding, third in the Open Championship, and reached the semi-finals of the Match-Play Championship.

Golf Illustrated – 3 October 1957

In 1959, Eric went to Palm Desert, California and was once more on the losing side in his Ryder Cup foursomes at the Eldorado Club, but he crushed Cary Middlecoff by four and three. This made him the only singles winner in the British side and he maintained his unbeaten singles record.

Regardless of his capricious personality, Brown was always a natural selection to be captain of the Ryder Cup team and he was given that honour (non-playing) in 1969, the historic tied match at Royal Birkdale Golf Club in Southport. The result was a great morale booster for British golf, which was in a state of expectation following Tony Jacklin's Open Championship win earlier that summer.

In 1960 and 1962, Brown took the British Match Play Championship. He was victorious in several European Opens, including the Swiss, Italian and Portuguese. He was runner-up in the Los Angeles Open of 1960 and continued to win tournaments in the late 1960s.

A few of Brown's comments just before the 1969 Ryder Cup failed to endear him to the Americans. The media reported that he had instructed the British team not to help their opponents search for their balls in the rough. Brown was not altogether polite, particularly in a game in which it is considered good form to assist one's rival in such a manner. But the visitors were at least a little placated when Brown explained that he did not want a British player running the risk of treading on an American ball and thereby losing a hole.

In the 1971 Ryder Cup, Brown was again the non-playing captain. He had played in the Cup in 1953, 1955, 1957 and 1959 and his record of four wins and four losses is a testament to his fighting qualities.

In 1971, Great Britain and Ireland were defeated at Old Warson Country Club in St Louis, but by a margin of just five points out of a possible 32, and as such this was the best result achieved by a Great Britain and Ireland team in the USA. The performance confirmed Brown as a formidable leader. Neil Coles, who had played more Ryder Cup matches than any other European, named Brown the finest captain he had served under.

Brown always rose to the challenge of the man-to-man combat of match-play. But his record in stroke-play, for such a talented golfer, was not nearly as good as many of his generation. But his Ryder Cup achievements give him a place in the chronicles of golf that many of his contemporaries would envy. Eric Brown is a major figure in the history of the great transatlantic fixture.

TOURNAMENTS AND AWARDS
1946 Scottish Amateur
1951 Swiss Open
1952 Italian Open
1953 Irish Open, Portuguese Open
1957 Dunlop Masters, Harry Vardon Trophy
1959 Golf Writers' Association Trophy
1960 *News of the World* Match Play
1962 *News of the World* Match Play

TOP-20 FINISHES IN THE OPEN	
3rd	1957
3rd=	1958
5th=	1961
9th=	1952, 1953, 1960
12th=	1955
17th=	1965
16th=	1969
18th=	1968

Harry Bradshaw, 43, from Portmarnock, has not had one of his best seasons. He tied for the Open Championship with Bobby Locke in 1949, but lost the play-off. Won the Dunlop Masters' title in 1953 and 1955 and played in the last two Ryder Cup matches.

Golf Illustrated – 3 October 1957

In the 1958 Canada Cup, Bradshaw, with Christy O'Connor as his partner, had one of his finest victories. The event was staged in Mexico City at a height of over 7,000 feet. The physical toll on the players was significant but Bradshaw, at 45 and a portly 15 stone, suffered more than most. The Irish pair won the team event ahead of some fabulous partnerships, including Brown and Panton, Snead and Hogan, and Player and Henning. Bradshaw also tied for the individual prize with Angel Miguel of Spain. Although he was defeated in the play-off, Harry rated his Canada Cup success above all else. He had struggled through the heat and the altitude and put Irish golf on the world map.

In his later life, Bradshaw was the professional at the renowned Portmarnock Club near Dublin. He was a storyteller of the highest quality and, until his passing in 1990, he was the father figure of Irish golf. A warm person with a relaxed manner, he was widely admired and respected. For the decade following World War II, he was Ireland's best golfer and, on the world stage, he helped promote Irish golf to a new level.

Harry dominated the Irish professional scene for the best part of 20 years and in the process became a household name across the Emerald Isle. He might be understood as the link between Fred Daly and Christy O'Connor. For Henry Longhurst, 'Bradshaw is my ideal golfer ... successful but completely unspoiled; approachable on the course and affable and good-humoured off it, still managing to keep golf a game while making it his business.'

Harry Weetman, 36-year-old Selsdon Park professional, has won two major tournaments this season – the Swallow Penfold and the German Open – and has also suffered from a back ailment. A member of the Ryder Cup team on the last three occasions, Weetman was Match-Play Champion in 1951 and runner-up last season. Represented England in the Canada Cup in 1953, 1954 and 1956.

Golf Illustrated – 3 October 1957

In 1959, the Great Britain and Ireland team travelled to the Eldorado Club, California. Although he had said he would never be captained by Dai Rees again, Harry Weetman, under skipper Rees, was paired in the foursomes with Dave Thomas, who was often able to hit the ball even further than Weetman. On the 36th tee, they were one hole up on the awesome pairing of Sam Snead and Cary Middlecoff, and, with the visitors' ball a long way down the middle from a Thomas drive, 'Slammin' Sam' splashed the American ball into the lake that defended the green. This meant that Middlecoff and Snead would not be able to do better than a five; a calmly struck short iron to the verge of the water, a pitch and two putts would guarantee Great Britain and Ireland one crucial point. But, without hesitation, Weetman grabbed a 5-iron and went straight for the green. With a horrible predictability, the ball plopped into the water and eventually Weetman and Thomas holed out in six strokes; Snead sank a long putt to win the hole and falter a half. It was a terrible blunder, even given Weetman's penchant for spurning the play-safe options. To add insult to injury, Weetman was badly beaten by Bob Rosburg in the singles.

At Lytham in 1961, Weetman was again prey to extraordinary circumstance. He was selected for just the two singles matches that were now contested over 18 holes. He had a putt on the 18th green to win the match against Doug Ford but missed it. He also missed the putt back and so lost the match. Facing Art Wall, Weetman went to the turn in 33 strokes; however, he was two down and Wall held on to claim victory by one hole.

Weetman's last playing appearance in the Ryder Cup was at East Lake, Atlanta, in 1963. He played in five matches but only managed one and a half points; however, he did beat Julius Boros in the first of the singles. Harry was the non-playing captain at Birkdale in 1965. Ironically, Dai Rees provided match commentary for television.

Weetman plied his trade in America, Australia, Africa, Canada, the Far East and in Europe. His use of power made him unpredictable but also an imperious presence that both attracted and excited spectators and he brought a great deal of life to British golf in the grey days of the 1950s. Although he had a bellicose demeanour on the greens, there was a kind of frank ingenuousness about Harry Weetman that, given a chance, he was able to express in a warm and engaging way away from the golf. As such, his death in a car accident in 1972 was a great loss for the character of golf in Britain.

Ken Bousfield, 38, has had only one notable success this season – a win in the Dunlop Tournament. But Bousfield

has shown consistency since his first professional win –
the Southern Assistants' title in 1947. Bousfield was a
Ryder Cup player in 1949, 1951 and 1955. Chief
successes: 1955 Match-Play Championship; 1955
National Close Championship. Represented England in
1956 Canada Cup.

Golf Illustrated – 3 October 1957

In 1959, Ken Bousfield took the German Open, for the
second time, and in the same year, at the Eldorado Country
Club, he lost his two Ryder Cup matches; in his singles he had
no answer to Mike Souchak's power, even though he covered
the initial nine holes after lunch in 32 shots, to go from five
down to two down. In 1961, with his customary partner, Dai
Rees, he won one foursomes and lost the other; in the singles,
he was beaten by Billy Casper, but won against Jerry Barber.

Bousfield's resolve and calmness under intense pressure
earned him a good record in the Ryder Cup and served him
well in his career on the British circuit. He triumphed in the
Portuguese Open in 1960 and retained that title in 1961. It
was also in 1961 that he won the Swallow-Penfold
tournament. Bousfield gained the British Seniors title in
1972; however, he was beaten in the World Seniors play-off
by Sam Snead.

Bousfield was well past his best years by the time the formal
European Tour came into being in 1972, but he played on the
Tour until 1976. He remained at the Coombe Hill Club
throughout his career. His dedication was concisely summed
up by golf writer Pat Ward-Thomas when he said, 'It is

refreshing sometimes to walk a few holes with him, for no other reason than to absorb a little of the soothing quality of his play and his company.'

Bousfield won the first PGA Championship at Pannal in 1955. The prize money was £500, but he recalled, 'You could buy a very good car for that in those days, even a flat.'

In the mid-1990s, approaching his 80th year, Bousfield could hardly believe the trimmings that accompany big tournaments, and was saddened by the somewhat austere expressions on the faces of many players. 'I suppose it's the ridiculous money,' he said.

Bousfield kept himself fit by going up to Coombe Hill every day for just a few holes by himself and occasionally driving to West Chiltington, or West Sussex, which he preferred, for a game with his old Ryder Cup team-mate Max Faulkner.

Ken Bousfield was one of the great exponents of the short game and late in life continued to possess a fine touch. He had lost count of the number of times he had beaten his age.

Max Faulkner, 41-year-old Selsey professional, has represented Britain in all post-war Ryder Cup matches save the last one. Open Champion in 1951. He finished third in the National Close Championship. He won the 1951 Dunlop Masters, the 1953 Match-Play Championship, and the 1951 and 1952 Dunlop Tournament.

Golf Illustrated – 3 October 1957

In 1968, at the age of 52, Max Faulkner took the Portuguese Open. This success was at least partly due to Faulkner's high level of fitness that he maintained throughout his life (although he was a committed smoker). But this was to be Faulkner's last major win. However, he won the Teacher British Senior Professional Championship at Aldeburgh the same year and repeated the feat in 1970 before retiring from tournament play.

Faulkner did not hit a golf ball again for almost two decades and concentrated on his lifelong passion for sea-fishing, especially for bass. He had an adventurous background in this sport; in 1950, he was fishing off Selsey, Sussex, and went to rescue two boys. He dived into the sea to save the lads who were being swept away by the current. In 1990, when he was asked if he would be watching the Open at St Andrews, he answered, 'I would rather be out in the boat catching some bream.'

Faulkner owned a farm in West Sussex where he retired to keep chickens and enjoy life as a gentleman farmer. He cherished the outdoor life. He had a great knowledge of nature and was able to recognise the bird calls he heard around his countryside habitat. However, he came back to the game at West Chiltington Golf Club, West Sussex, of which he was half owner. It opened in 1988, and is situated just over the hill from his farmhouse home in Pulborough. The former Open Champion could often be seen advancing across the fairways dressed like a vagabond, shovel in hand, with a set of mole traps draped over his shoulder. He would sometimes offer golfing tips to those on the course, although few had any idea who he was.

Apart from his overseas exhibition tours, Faulkner travelled all over Britain, giving clinics and exhibition matches in aid of the Cancer Relief Fund. In his lifetime, he probably played more charity golf matches than most professional golfers. Shortly before his passing, Faulkner asked for those who might have purchased wreaths for his funeral to make donations to the Macmillan Cancer Relief charity. In all his journeying, he charmed all he met with his personality and humour.

Faulkner's fervour for golf was a consistent feature in his life. He was the author of two books – *The Faulkner Method* (1952) and *Play Championship Golf All Your Life* (1972). He set up one of the first programmes for coaching aspiring young professionals, the Butten Scheme that was designed, via first-class coaching, fitness and diet, to create British golfers able to compete on the world stage. Alongside others, it produced Tommy Horton and Brian Barnes, who were amongst the most successful Butten Boys. They both became Ryder Cup players, and the Scotsman Barnes went on to design the West Chiltington Golf Club, and married Max's daughter Hilary.

In 1995 at Portrush, Faulkner watched his son-in-law win the Senior British Open. It must have been a great boost for Barnes and the Faulkner family as Brian had been struggling with alcoholism before the mid-1990s when he returned to the Seniors Tour.

At the age of 86, Faulkner became an official PGA Tour winner. Thanks to a policy change by the Tour, all British Open victories prior to 1995 were to be counted as official PGA Tour victories. As such, Faulkner's 1951 Open win counted as an official PGA Tour win. Faulkner responded to the news saying, 'Good God, really? Well, it's about time.'

At the end of 2001, Faulkner received an OBE for his services to golf and was made a Freeman of the City of London.

Many saw the very late recognition of Faulkner's inclusion in the New Year's honours list as at best well overdue and at worst evidence that he had been previously 'blackballed' by those who ruled the darker corridors of the golf hierarchy and made to pay the price for flouting their pomposity from the mid-1940s on. For around 10 years, the European Tour and PGA had been working to get Faulkner's contribution officially recognised, and, although he didn't once complain about waiting for an honour, the members at West Chiltington never hid their agitation at his being so long overlooked.

When the acknowledgement finally came, Faulkner was elated and touchingly grateful: 'I am very patriotic and, when I go to Buckingham Palace to receive it, I shall tell the Queen that I hope she reigns for longer than Queen Victoria did.'

The Faulkner clan were also delighted. Hilary, his daughter, told how the family were 'absolutely thrilled'. Brian Barnes said, 'Max is chuffed. There is no doubt about that but, at the same time, he is pretty nonplussed and a little surprised that it should have come after all this time.'

Until a year before his death, Faulkner still played nine holes in 36 strokes at West Chiltington. At that time, he had no part in the ownership of the course as the business was bought by Geoffrey Cotton. Faulkner would politely refuse offers from Cotton to use an electric buggy; not only did he prefer to walk but he carried his own bag over a course that is by no means flat.

Faulkner celebrated the 50th anniversary of his Open win by giving his gold medal to the Professional Golf Association for their archives.

Max Faulkner passed away on Saturday, 26 February 2005, at the age of 88 following a heart attack. The galleries of the game loved him, as evidenced by the huge number of letters of condolence the Faulkner family has received from all over the world.

Along with Henry Cotton (1948), Tony Jacklin (1969), Sandy Lyle (1985), Nick Faldo (1987, 1990, 1992) and Paul Lawrie (1999), he was one of the half-dozen British golfers to have won the Open Championship since World War II.

According to Brian Barnes, 'Max was the first great entertainer in British golf. And what made him such a great entertainer was that he had the game to go with it. He was a superb striker of the ball and had a wonderful golf swing. He was always super-confident. I don't think I ever heard him utter a negative thought. He always thought positively. He used to say, if you think you are lucky, you will be.'

Faulkner's passing cut a tie with a more charming age when golf was packed with personalities. He once said, 'Golf has been good to me and I like to think that I've given something to the game.' He most certainly did.

Peter Alliss, 26, won the National Close Championship at Llandudno. He finished second in the Spalding Tournament and was joint second in the Swallow and Penfold. He won the 1954 Daks Tournament and last year's Spanish Open. Alliss played for Britain in the 1953 Ryder Cup match.

Golf Illustrated – 3 October 1957

Peter Alliss was to wait until 1959 for his first Ryder Cup victory, alongside Christy O'Connor, in the foursomes in California. He halved his singles with Jay Hebert and was the only undefeated British player.

In the four Ryder Cups from 1959 to 1965, Alliss won nine and halved four of his 18 games in a period when Britain were defeated in every tie.

Alliss was to be amongst the most outstanding British golfers from the late 1950s to the end of the 1960s. In three consecutive weeks in 1958, he was triumphant in the Spanish, Italian and Portuguese Opens; he won the Dunlop Masters (again) in 1959, the PGA Close Championship three times and the Martini; and he was awarded the Vardon Trophy in 1964 and 1966.

Thought by numerous commentators and fellow professionals to be the finest striker of a golf ball the UK had to offer, Alliss was unable to perfect his putting. As almost a last resort, he took to a cross-handed method, but this did not prove to be the answer to his problems.

Notwithstanding his frustration at Wentworth in 1953 (where he lost both his foursomes and singles), Alliss consistently appeared to be a better performer when he played for his country. He twice met Arnold Palmer in the Ryder Cup and beat him in one match and halved the other. Alliss was never to forget that battle (his first meeting with Palmer) in 1961 at Lytham. It included some superb shot-making by both players and the two men were applauded right the way along the last fairway, as if it were the Open Championship (Palmer was never to beat Alliss in Ryder Cup singles).

As well as Palmer, Alliss beat Billy Casper and Ken Venturi in Ryder Cup singles matches. In foursomes and fourball matches, Alliss was particularly successful when paired with Christy O'Connor, a player for whom the Englishman had tremendous respect.

In 1962, Alliss repeatedly attempted to challenge the image of club professionals being the lowest form of golf life when he was captain of the Professional Golfers' Association. Like many other players, he had long experienced being thought of as no more than a sort of low-grade servant rather than the valuable asset he was. For example, in 1958, he won the Spanish, Portuguese and Italian Open titles within a month and returned victorious to his Parkstone club, only to be confronted by a furious member who asked, 'Where have you been? I've been waiting three weeks for a lesson.'

Alliss won five points out of six in the Ryder Cup of 1965; his one loss was in a fourball match against Palmer and Dave Marr. In 1969, Alliss made his final appearance in the Ryder Cup at Royal Birkdale. He recollected being defeated in the morning singles by Lee Trevino, having become very unsteady on the greens. He thought that he had bettered the American and was inside his ball on eight or nine of the greens; however, Peter lost two and one. Alliss asked to be omitted from the afternoon matches. The Americans were held to a draw, Britain's best result for a dozen years.

Alliss represented England in the Canada/World Cup from 1954 to 1959 and again in 1961, 1962, 1966 and 1967. In 1987, Alliss was made PGA captain for a second time.

As the 1970s peeped over the horizon, Alliss started his

long television career, taking over from Henry Longhurst at the BBC. His sophisticated, well-informed and sometimes idiosyncratic observations made his dulcet tones synonymous with golf. He has published many books (including a novel). He has also made numerous videos/DVDs and is known as a fine after-dinner speaker.

Alliss has been involved in golf-course architecture and design for many years with the likes of Dave Thomas and Clive Clark. His single regret is never being asked to captain a Ryder Cup team.

Peter Alliss has had a long and honourable career in professional golf and to many he is, through the power of television, the voice of the modem game.

TOURNAMENTS AND AWARDS
1954 Daks
1955 Dunlop Professional
1956 Spanish Open
1957 PGA Close Championship
1958 Italian, Portuguese and Spanish Opens
1959 Dunlop Professional
1962 PGA Close Championship
1963 Daks (shared with NC Coles)
1964 Harry Vardon Trophy
1965 PGA Close Championship and headed Order of Merit Points table
1966 Harry Vardon Trophy
1967 Agfa-Gevaert
1969 Piccadilly Match Play

Peter Mills, the 26-year-old Pinner Hill professional, was the last man to win his Ryder Cup place. This will be his first Ryder Cup match. Mills won the Coombe Hill Assistants' Tournament in 1951 and 1953, was joint second in last year's Daks Tournament and third in the Dunlop.

Golf Illustrated – 3 October 1957

Peter Mills won a place in the 1959 Ryder Cup team but picked up a back injury during a practice round and was unable to play.

Mills reached the semi-final of the PGA Match Play Championship in 1956. His single major win was in the Bowmaker tournament of 1958. Ultimately, Mills applied for and received reinstatement as an amateur and slipped into obscurity.

CHAPTER NINETEEN

Burke's Boys

The American team learned a lot from their Lindrick experience as did US golf. They had let themselves be made vulnerable, and the Ryder Cup of 1959 demonstrated that they had digested the lesson and the gloves were off. The domination of American golf over the era that followed has much to do with what happened in Yorkshire in 1957. The men that carried the new awareness and understanding back across the Atlantic had fascinating careers in the decades that followed their collective defeat.

Art Wall, Jun., 33, a consistent player who is seldom out of the money. This season he won the Pensacola Open. His most notable achievement was winning the Tournament of Champions at Las Vegas, Nevada, in

1954. He has developed a habit of being on form in odd years – and this is 1957.

Golf Illustrated – 3 October 1957

Bob Goalby, a regular fellow traveller and long-term friend of Wall recalled how, in 1959, the year Art won the Crosby, the two men travelled down to San Diego. They were out on the greens together and Art made one. Goalby marvelled at his friend's ability to consistently hole in one. Art's explanation was that he made the hole the target of every shot he made, but it was said with more irony than gravity.

Wall was selected PGA Tour Player of the Year in 1959 with four victories. Prize money of $53,167 made him the Tour's top earner and he was awarded the Vardon Trophy, all of which made that last year of the 1950s Art's best. The highpoint of that season and his career came on 5 April at the end of the 23rd Golf Masters Championship at the Augusta National.

In the late 1950s, during Masters Week in Augusta, most visitors rented private homes. This still happens, but in those days there were only three hotels of any note. Downtown was the old and, for Augusta, historic Great Pyramid Richmond. Nearer the course, on Walton Way, and directly opposite each other, there were the almost equally antiquated Leaning Tower of Bon Air and the Petrified Forest Partridge Inn, which has in recent years been renovated and is currently one of the more fashionable venues in the district.

The year of Art Wall's Masters Triumph, his only career win in a Major championship, these places had a number of common traits. The lights in the rooms would go out a moment after you'd turned them on and the water running into the bathrooms came in a range of hues, from a flushed rosy colour to robust orange or even light rust brown. Room service was organised on a kind of postal roster, you had to order a day or so in advance of a delivery date. Even then, if you ordered a burger you'd be more likely to get salad. Of course, things have changed. Now you are sure to get a burger.

At the start of the final round, Wall was six shots behind Stan Leonard and the defending champion Arnold Palmer. Wall was five strokes behind Cary Middlecoff with seven holes to play. However, on the Sunday, Wall passed 12 players on the leader board to claim the green jacket, having birdied five of his last six holes, to close with a 66 (shooting 284), one stroke ahead of Middlecoff and two ahead of Palmer. It was to be remembered as being among the biggest final-round comebacks in the history of the Masters. Wall told his son, Greg, who has been head pro at Pocono Manor Golf Club since 1984, that he 'caught lightning in a bottle that day'.

In that same year at Eldorado, Wall and Doug Ford lost to Christy O'Connor and Peter Alliss, but Wall won his first Ryder Cup point and a decisive victory over O'Connor. In his final appearance in the Cup in 1961, Wall took three points out of three at Lytham. Two of the matches were determined on the final green. Alongside Jay Hebert, Wall made a birdie, to beat his old adversaries, O'Connor and Alliss, in the foursomes; in the singles, Wall was involved in a marvellous confrontation with Harry Weetman. The Brit got round the first nine holes in 33 strokes, but Wall was two up, only having needed 31 shots. Over the last nine holes, Wall was just able to keep in front and won by one hole.

Wall was the consummate professional on the golf course, but he concealed a sharp sense of humour, although he was often funny when he wasn't trying to be humorous. Wall's partner on the old CBS Golf Classic in the 1960s, Charles Coody, remembered his 1967 struggle with Billy Casper for the Canadian Open Championship in Montreal. A successful 20-foot putt gave Wall a birdie at the 16th hole. As Wall strode towards the 17th tee, a fan called out, 'Way to go, Art. Let's get two more birdies and then you can give us a big smile.'

Without breaking his stride, Wall turned to the spectator and commented, 'Sir, if this were a smiling contest, I wouldn't have entered.'

Wall's professionalism extended beyond the greens. According to Goalby, while other players were ready to go out drinking after a day on the course, Wall was happy with Oreo cookies and a pint of milk in his room.

At the 1964 San Diego Open, Wall met the ostentatious Tony Lema for the Championship. Following the round on the Saturday, Lema promised each member of the press tent audience a bottle of champagne if he won the next day. Wall told the same group that, if *he* won, he'd get everybody a pint of milk. Wall *did* win on the Sunday and everyone in the press tent received a pint of milk, which probably says a great deal about the man.

Wall was not particularly verbose, but to both other players and members of the public he was certainly a very nice, friendly, helpful and courteous person, who let his game do the talking for him. Despite his success, he never sought publicity or notoriety and seemed happier out of the limelight, being modest and apparently uncomfortable when too much attention was paid to him. He was a family man devoted to his wife Jean and their five children.

For Charles Coody, Wall was the 'salt of the earth', and one would not find a better individual in golf. He recollected how, in 1964, Coody's first year, Wall had introduced himself, although Coody knew who he was. But Wall told the Masters winner of 1971 from Stamford, Texas, that he would do anything he could to help him.

In 1965, Wall claimed the Augusta course record of 20; it was equalled by Gay Brewer, in 1973.

The former Senior PGA Tour player Dick Hendrickson also admired Wall's obliging nature. As a young assistant pro at the Country Club of Scranton, he was impressed with Wall's game when he first got to know him. At the time, Hendrickson recognised himself to be erratic, but he confessed to never having seen anybody hit a ball so straight and so accurate with so much control. Hendrickson rarely made a putt back then, but Wall helped him with that side of his game.

In the early 1970s, Wall was still hitting as far and as straight as many top players and putts found the hole as if attracted by a kind of magnetism. He could birdie nine holes in the mid-1960s with what seemed like consummate ease and left many of those who watched him unable to understand why he didn't defeat the likes of Lee Trevino and Jack Nicklaus on a regular basis.

Wall loved to play golf in the place he grew up, Scranton Country Club and at Honesdale, and not too many days went by without him picking up his clubs.

In his career, Wall won 14 times on the PGA Tour, including the 1975 Greater Milwaukee Open, two months off his 52nd birthday, which made him the second-oldest Tour Champion in history. It was his final tournament win as an individual. His last victory was teaming with Tommy Bolt to win the 1980 Legends of Golf on the Senior PGA Tour, but he continued to play at the highest level up to 1988 and would rarely miss a day on the greens for the rest of his life.

At the tail-end of his career, Wall appeared in a televised series of matches, *USA v The World*. He was unfortunate to come up against Christy O'Connor on a links course in Britain with the wind blowing a gale and the rain pouring down. O'Connor thrived in the conditions and made a score of under 70. Wall looked a doleful figure as the rain dripped from him, obviously filled with the desire to be anywhere but where he was; he only just broke 80.

A member of the Philadelphia Section of the PGA, Wall often returned to play in the Philadelphia PGA Championship, and was victorious in that event on five occasions.

With the first stirrings of winter 2001, Wall was admitted to Mercy Hospital, Scranton, with pneumonia. Just under a month later, on Wednesday morning, 31 October, he died of respiratory failure. He was 77. A family man, Art was survived by his wife Jean Louise; two sons, three daughters, nine grandchildren and two great-grandchildren.

Golf and the world beyond the sport will remember Art Wall as a good person and a humble gentleman who loved the game and felt himself lucky to be successful at something he loved. He experienced a deep happiness every time he played.

Art Wall was a fine competitor and, as PGA Tour commissioner Tim Finchem said, 'He will be missed by his fellow pros, but always remembered for his kind nature off the golf course and his accomplishments on it.'

PGA TOUR WINS
1953 (1) Fort Wayne Open
1954 (1) Tournament of Champions
1956 (1) Fort Wayne Open
1957 (1) Pensacola Open Invitational
1958 (2) Rubber City Open Invitational, Eastern Open Invitational
1959 (4) Bing Crosby National Pro-Am, Azalea Open Invitational, The Masters, Buick Open Invitational
1960 (1) Canadian Open
1964 (1) San Diego Open Invitational
1966 (1) Insurance City Open Invitational
1975 (1) Greater Milwaukee Open

Dick Mayer, 33, the man who broke through to win the US Open this year after a tie with Dr. Cary Middlecoff. Mayer, who was a well-known amateur in the New York area before turning pro, nearly won the 1954

Open. He spoilt his chances by taking a seven on the par 4 18th to finish third. He won the Tam O'Shanter World Tournament.

Golf Illustrated – 3 October 1957

In 1965, at the Lakewood Country Club, Dick Mayer made what some were to call the greatest shot in the history of the New Orleans Open to win this event by one shot over Bruce Devlin. Mayer's chip from 35 yards out snatched victory from Devlin, taking the $100,000 prize and beating a field that included Jack Nicklaus and Arnold Palmer.

Mayer's career was interrupted in 1969 by tendon problems and a broken elbow and he was never quite the redoubtable player he had been. But he picked up $50,000 for a hole in one at the Palm Springs Open in 1962 and, two years later, won the New Orleans Open.

Dick Mayer passed away in Palm Springs, California, on 2 June 1989.

PGA TOUR WINS
1953 Eastern Open
1954 Miami Beach International Four-Ball
(with Tommy Bolt)
1955 Kansas City Open
1956 Philadelphia Daily News Open
1957 US Open, World Championship of Golf
1965 Greater New Orleans Open Invitational

Doug Ford, 35, is having a wonderful year. He is leading the money winners by a lap (excluding the Tam O'Shanter), having won the Masters and the Los Angeles Open and being runner-up in the Wykagyl Round Robin and the Akron Open. He was the 1955 PGA Champion and annexed two points that year in the Ryder Cup match.

Golf Illustrated – 3 October 1957

After winning the Pensacola Open Invitational in 1958, Doug Ford said, 'This is a great victory for scramblers. There aren't many of us scrapers left.'

He was indeed a fighter. In the 1959 Ryder Cup at Eldorado, Ford and Art Wall were beaten by Christy O'Connor and Peter Alliss. In his singles match, Ford was four holes in front of Norman Drew at lunchtime, but the game was eventually halved. In his last appearance in the event at Lytham in 1961, Ford, alongside Gene Littler, was once more beaten by O'Connor and Alliss. But he unexpectedly won in his singles, beating Harry Weetman, who on the final green failed to sink a very short putt. However, in the second singles, Dai Rees easily beat Ford.

By the early 1960s, no other pro could match Ford's record and only three active tournament players, Sam Snead, Cary Middlecoff and Arnold Palmer, had won more tournaments than him. He was at that time considered one of the most durable professionals on the Tour.

Ford's self-assurance and skill with the pitching wedge was demonstrated in the final round of the New York

Metropolitan Open one year. On the 16th hole, he was five under par. He hooked his drive into the rough and, when he got to the ball, he was obliged to wait for an ambling threesome who were lining up putts on the green. Ford could have reached the green with a 5-iron, but, as was his habit, he had the urge to move swiftly on. Refusing to wait until the group ahead had putted out, Ford drew his wedge and deliberately played a 70-yard short for the green, seemingly sure he would be able to get down in two from there; he did – with a great wedge approach that almost hit the pin, and an easy tap-in putt for his par.

In 1961, Ford was playing as hard as ever, being involved in 29 events in the first nine months of the year. He was one of the most consistent and industrious professionals on the US Tour. The last of Ford's 19 PGA Tour wins was the Canadian Open of 1963, but he continued competing on Tour until the mid-1970s, usually finishing in the top 10 in any event for the best part of his career.

He was inducted into the Connecticut Golf Hall of Fame in 1972.

Ford, who last made the halfway cut in 1971 and last broke 80 in 1993, returned an opening 94 in 2000 before quitting. He withdrew after only a few holes in April 2001.

In 2002, Ford let the world know that, along with 1967 winner Gay Brewer and 1970 winner Billy Casper, he would not be playing on the Masters course in Augusta (which had been lengthened by nearly 300 yards since Tiger Woods won his second title).

Ford's career spanned a considerable period of time; he

made his last appearances in major tournaments in 1975 and went on to play on the Senior Tour.

To put Ford's longevity into perspective, Tiger Woods would have to play every year until 2043 to equal Ford's record.

Doug Ford's golf career was characterised by his intelligent approach to the game. In the 1960s, he published a book called *The Brainy Way to Better Golf*, which summed up his style and attitude perfectly.

PGA TOUR WINS
1952 (1) Jacksonville Open
1953 (3) Virginia Beach Open, Labatt Open, Miami Open
1954 (2) Greater Greensboro Open, Fort Wayne Open
1955 (3) All American Open, Carling Golf Classic, PGA Championship
1957 (3) Los Angeles Open, The Masters, Western Open
1958 (1) Pensacola Open Invitational
1959 (1) Canadian Open
1960 (1) '500' Festival Open Invitational
1961 (1) '500' Festival Open Invitational
1962 (2) Bing Crosby National Pro-Am, Eastern Open Invitational
1963 (1) Canadian Open

Dow Finsterwald, 27, is the most promising young pro on the circuit. He finished second money winner last season and is lying third this year. He was runner-up in the PGA

Championship, won the Tucson Open and has finished second in three other tournaments this season.

Golf Illustrated – 3 October 1957

In 1958, at Llanerch Country Club in Havertown, Pennsylvania, the PGA Championship format was changed to a stroke-play contest (it was the first year of the stroke/medal play). Dow Finsterwald began with a round of 67 to lead but really clinched matters when he went to the turn in his final round in 31. He won by two strokes from Billy Casper. Finsterwald was duly named as the PGA Player of the Year. He finished in the money in 72 consecutive tournaments making him second only to Byron Nelson's 113 consecutive cuts. This record stood for many years until it was eclipsed by Jack Nicklaus, Hale Irwin and Tiger Woods; however, he is still fifth on the list today. Finsterwald is pleased to claim that he is 'still in good company'.

Three and a half years after the PGA Championship at Llanerch, Finsterwald and Gary Player fought out one of the most epic battles in golf history – the Masters of 1962, at Augusta National. It was to be perhaps one of the most bittersweet times in Finsterwald's long pro career.

In 2006, Finsterwald recalled taking three from the very edge of the 17th hole for a bogey, which dropped him back to eight under and that was the tying score. It would have been at the top of his list of accomplishments had he won. But the bogey at 17 forced a play-off with Arnold Palmer and Gary Player.

Palmer remembered getting pretty hot on the back nine, recollecting how Finsterwald had shot himself out of it on the front nine. Palmer had a slow start, but caught Player on the back nine. The game concluded with Finsterwald shooting 77, Player 71 and Palmer 68.

After playing in four Ryder Cup teams (1957, 1959, 1961, 1963), Finsterwald was the non-playing captain of the 1977 US team that were victorious at Royal Lytham. His first outing in the Ryder Cup was the American defeat at Lindrick. But he was undefeated in 1959 at Eldorado, and in 1961 he got revenge for what was something of a grudge match with Christy O'Connor in 1957, when he beat the Irishman in the first singles. But Finsterwald lost to Neil Coles in the second series. His final appearance as a player was at East Lake, Atlanta, two years later. Finsterwald performed magnificently to score four wins and a half out of six games.

His record in the Ryder Cup shows that, of the 13 games he played, he won nine, lost three and halved one.

Finsterwald won 11 times on the PGA Tour during his career, although seven of those came in the three years from 1958 to 1960. (In the years 1956 to 1960, he was in the top-three money-winners on the US Tour, coming second in both 1956 and 1958.) A renowned perfectionist from tee to green, Finsterwald was considered one of the most consistent players on the Tour in the late 1950s and early 1960s.

With the emergence of Arnold Palmer (who was to become a close friend of Finsterwald's) with his bold play, Finsterwald's stratagem of hitting fairways and, from there, going for the safest shot to the greens looked distinctly one-dimensional. However, he was a superb putter. He had a similar approach to Bobby Locke and Peter Thomson, and he made it work. Finsterwald was never seen with a string of bogeys on his card. He was a very straight hitter from the tee, and some claimed that he considered a shot driven directly at the flag to be something of a failure. He wanted to play the right shot and was happy if he could fade in a high one or draw one low to the flag if he saw that was the perfect shot.

At one point, Finsterwald was seen by some as the natural heir to Ben Hogan, although he did not possess the genius of the 'Iron Man' from Texas. However, during his peak years, Finsterwald was one of the foremost players on the American Tour.

In 1969, he was inducted into the Ohio University Athletics Hall of Fame, joining his uncle, Russ Finsterwald, who was in the first class of inductees as a football and basketball player as well as a football head coach.

Finsterwald was once involved in litigation in which the plaintiff claimed she lost the sight in her right eye as a result of an errant tee-shot he hit at the 18th hole at the 1973 Western Open. A jury found Finsterwald not liable; however, Midlothian Country Club's insurers had to pay the woman about $450,000.

For Finsterwald, winning the PGA and being named Ryder Cup captain in 1977 are the high points in his golfing career. He played on the Tour until the mid-1970s and his steadiness never wavered.

Finsterwald can remember when professional golfers played in relative anonymity compared to today's glamour, money and popularity. But, looking back on first-place prizes of $2,000, while understanding that such sums went a lot further in those days, he was quick to make the point that they certainly did not spread as far as $1.8 million today.

According to Finsterwald, golf was fortunate to have a personality like Arnold Palmer, and Palmer was the right man at the right time and right place for golf. In return, Palmer admired Finsterwald, and often said that he was a great player, but also told how he was always nagging Finsterwald to be more aggressive, although Palmer understood that he had a plan and he stuck with it.

Finsterwald's one regret is not playing in the British Open. At a time when the Americans travelled to Europe by ship, he confessed to being lured by the options of bigger prize money in the USA when the standard of his play was high enough to warrant taking on the challenge offered in Britain. He admitted to being more mercenary than he might have been. But, for all this, for Finsterwald, life as a pro golfer was a joy.

There is a plaque in his honour at the putting green at the Broadmoor Golf Club in Colorado Springs where he was the director of golf for 28 years, bringing national attention to the club. Unfortunately, he took up his post on 22 November 1963, the day President Kennedy was assassinated in Dallas, and naturally the planned ceremony was cut short in the circumstances.

Having served as PGA Vice-President from 1976 to 1978, and on the USGA Rules of Golf committee from 1979 to 1981, as he neared his 80th birthday, having been involved in golf all his life, Finsterwald had an encyclopaedic knowledge of the game. He saw Bobby Jones play only on film, but sees himself as bridging eras in golfing history. For Finsterwald, players such as Nelson, Jones, Ben Hogan, Player, Nicklaus and Palmer would be winners at any point in time. But he saw Sam Snead as amazing, winning tournaments at 53 years of age.

Of Tiger Woods, Finsterwald has said that he sees no limit to how far he can go, although he thinks that Tiger will have more quality players to beat. According to Finsterwald, the tournament fields today are much deeper than the fields he was asked to compete in.

Today he lives in Orlando during the winter and Colorado Springs during the summer with his wife, Linda. They have three sons and a daughter, and five grandchildren. His middle son, Dow Junior, is head pro at the Colonial Country Club in Fort Worth, Texas, site of the Bank of America Colonial.

Dow Finsterwald remains active in the golfing community, currently serving as a member of the Masters tournament board. He still plays in a few tournaments over the year, and there's a good chance he might be found on the practice green each morning at the Broadmoor during the summer months.

PGA TOUR WINS
1955 (1) Fort Wayne Invitational
1956 (1) Carling Open Invitational
1957 (1) Tucson Open Invitational
1958 (2) PGA Championship, Utah Open Invitational
1959 (3) Greater Greensboro Open, Carling Open Invitational, Kansas City Open Invitational
1960 (2) Los Angeles Open, Greater New Orleans Open Invitational
1963 (1) '500' Festival Open Invitational

Ed Furgol, 40, winner of the 1954 Open, has gained his place on his consistency. He competed in the 1955 British Open at St Andrews when he proved himself a very popular visitor.

Golf Illustrated – 3 October 1957

In his rare appearances after 1957, Ed Furgol was still a formidably resolute player and, at the 1963 Masters, for example, at the start of the final round he was just one behind Jack Nicklaus, the eventual winner.

After a brief illness, Ed died in Miami Shores, Florida on 6 March 1997.

PGA TOUR WINS
1947 (1) Bing Crosby Pro-Am (tie with George Fazio)
1954 (2) Phoenix Open, US Open
1956 (2) Miller High Life Open, Rubber City Open
1957 (1) Agua Caliente Open

Fred Hawkins, 34, is a player who seldom hits the headlines, but managed to finish fourth money winner in 1956. He is well up among the leaders again this year, although his best effort was finishing second in the Eastern Open.

Golf Illustrated – 3 October 1957

Hawkins tied for second in the 1958 Masters and still tees up occasionally at Spring Valley. He reached the quarter-finals of the US PGA Championship twice and tied for second place behind Arnold Palmer in the 1958 Masters.

> Ted Kroll, 38, biggest money winner in 1956 by virtue of winning the Tam O'Shanter Tournament, which has kept him off the circuit most of this season. He played in the 1953 and 1955 teams, winning two out of a possible three points, being beaten 9 and 7 by Fred Daly in 1953.
>
> *Golf Illustrated* – 3 October 1957

During the 1960s, Ted won seven tournaments on the American circuit, including the San Diego, Tucson and Houston Opens, and the money-spinning World Championship of Golf. His final victory was in the Canadian Open of 1962.

Ted was married for over 50 years and had four daughters. In his later years he suffered from Parkinson's disease. He died in Boca Raton, Florida, on 23 April 2002.

PGA TOUR WINS
1952 (2) San Diego Open, Insurance City Open
1953 (1) National Celebrities Open
1955 (1) Philadelphia Daily News Open
1956 (3) Tucson Open Invitational, Houston Open, World Championship of Golf
1962 (1) Canadian Open

Lionel Hebert, 29, is the younger brother of the better-known Jay Hebert; he came from 'nowhere' to win the PGA Championship and assured himself of an automatic place in the team.

Golf Illustrated – 3 October 1957

Lionel Hebert won the Tucson Open in 1958 and the Memphis Open in 1962. Hebert won six PGA Tour titles during a career in which he and his brother, Jay, became the most successful pair of brothers on the Tour.

A lifelong resident of Lafayette, following his retirement, Hebert worked as a golf instructor. He served as National Vice-President of the PGA of America twice and as chairman of its Tournament Committee in 1962–63 and 1972–73.

Lionel died at his home in Lafayette, Louisiana on 30 December 2000, aged 72.

After his death, Lionel Hebert's family requested that memorial contributions in his name be made to the Kidney Foundation of Louisiana and the American Diabetes Association.

PGA TOUR WINS
1956 St Petersburg Open
1957 PGA Championship
1958 Tucson Open Invitational
1960 Cajun Classic
1962 Memphis Open Invitational
1966 Florida Citrus Open Invitational

Tommy Bolt, 38, is a controversial figure on the course, but one of the most liked pros on the circuit. He won the fourth tournament in his six years as a tournament pro in July – the Eastern Open. In the 1955 matches he won both his foursome and single.

Golf Illustrated – 3 October 1957

Tommy Bolt managed to hold his temper at Southern Hills in the 1958 US Open. He was smiling most of the week, joking with the press and the gallery. The rough was so high that, if a player missed the fairway, a sand wedge was needed to get him out. His demeanour was unusually convivial, but it seems that the heatwave weather suited him. It was 95 degrees and humid with winds of 15 to 20 miles per hour. When it's like that in Tulsa, the indolent zephyrs carry a tang of petroleum. To those not acclimatised to it, such conditions can induce a kind of vague nausea. But this was Bolt's home state, and he was used to it.

Most of the other competitors were wilting and growing tired. But Bolt was in his element. After a birdie on the 1st hole, he turned to the press and said, 'I wonder who'll finish second?'

Coming down the stretch he was so laidback he was playing to the gallery. He birdied Southern Hills' treacherous 12th hole three consecutive times. On the last hole, an extremely difficult par 4, Bolt was on the fairway with the ball a foot and a half below him. He had around 220 yards in front of him. Bolt whipped out his little 5-wood and just sailed it right up on the green.

Recalling that tournament, Bolt told of how at that time there was a 36-hole finish on the Saturday. There was no play on Sunday because that was the 'Lord's Day'. But, Bolt observed, seven years later, the USGA and television discovered there was a lot of money to be made on the Lord's Day, and that was the end of the 36-hole finish.

Victory in the Masters had been something of the pinnacle of a comeback for Bolt.

If the Seniors had come about by the end of 1960s, Bolt would have been a dominant figure on that Tour. However, he did win the National Seniors Association Open five times in succession from 1968 to 1972 and in 1969 won the US Seniors. Later, in 1969, Bolt won the World Seniors, defeating John Panton on the 39th hole. In 1971, at the age of 53, he was tied with Jack Nicklaus with nine holes left, but finished third in the US PGA Championship. At the 10th in the final round, Bolt hit a 4-wood about 15 feet past the hole, then holed it for a birdie. But he could only shoot even par over the last nine. Nicklaus shot three under and beat Bolt by three. But Nicklaus was playing the best golf of his life.

Bolt's honours in Senior titles in the US and Australia run into double figures. He was one of the pioneers of the Champions Tour, laying the groundwork in a memorable six-hole sudden-death play-off with partner Art Wall against Julius Boros and Roberto De Vicenzo in the 1979 Legends of Golf, won by Boros and De Vicenzo.

At the end of the 70s, Bolt was still winning Seniors events and playing the occasional invitation tournament on the

European Tour, and he won the Australian Seniors in both 1978 and 1979.

The 1980 Liberty Mutual Legends of Golf tournament gave Senior golf another lift when the 'odd couple' of the game, Bolt and Wall, returned and fired a six-under-par 64 on the final day for a Legends' record 23 under-par total score of 187 to win the event.

Bolt tied for fourth place in the Masters of 1961. His final Masters was 1972, when he missed the cut.

Despite his histrionics, a number of which were overstated and others contrived by himself, Bolt was a golfer of the highest class. He was (and continues to be) a vibrant character who added some welcome flamboyance to the game and he liked to please the gallery. He understood that it 'thrills crowds to see a guy suffer. That's why I threw clubs so often.' He told of how he knew the spectators loved to see golf get the better of the players, and confessed that he was only too happy to oblige them. Bolt admitted that at first he threw clubs because he was irritated. But after a time 'heaving irons' became something of a gimmick or his personal 'catchphrase'. He told of how he learned, 'If you helicopter those dudes by throwing them sideways instead of overhand, you could avoid breaking the shaft.'

Bolt claimed to have turned his party piece into an art form over the years, which could be backed up by his ironic observation that the driver goes the shortest distance when you throw it, while the putter flies furthest, followed by the sand wedge.

But, for those who watched Bolt and followed his career, it was obvious that, if he had been able to control his temper and raised his putting game, he would have probably had a much more impressive record in major championships. Indeed, Ben Hogan believed that, if Bolt could have handled his emotions better and dealt with failure, he might have had no equal. Hogan once said, 'If we could've screwed another head on his shoulders, Tommy Bolt could have been the greatest who ever played.'

But this was never going to happen. He once had a good go at jamming a top-playing colleague's tam o'shanter down his throat, and occurrences of this type were far more likely than his developing some brand of 'instant karma'.

Bolt is one of the two 1957 Ryder Cup players that have been elected into the World Golf Hall of Fame. The other was Jack Burke Jr in 2000. Bolt was inducted in the veterans' category on Wednesday, 15 November 2002, at the World Golf Village in St Augustine, Florida, along with Bernhard Langer, Ben Crenshaw, Tony Jacklin and Marlene Hagge of the LPGA Tour, bringing the Hall of Fame membership to 94 (19 more players have been inducted since 2002).

The 84-year-old Bolt thought it was 'unbelievable' and said that he was very proud to be in the Hall of Fame, but he did think he should have been in long before 2002, and that his exclusion had been 'political'. For years, Bolt was critical of the Senior PGA Tour, especially the way it seemed to take care of the younger Seniors but not the older players like him. According to Bolt, the moment he stopped complaining, he got elected, illustrating: 'You attract more flies with honey than with vinegar.'

Bolt was not affronted by his nicknames like 'Thunder Bolt' or 'Terrible Tommy'. He once said, 'People recognised me for who I am – a golfer showing my emotions.'

During the first decade of the 21st century, at the magnificent Quarry Course at the Black Diamond Ranch Golf and Country Club in Lecanto, Florida, Bolt still played nine holes a day. He didn't rise too early in the mornings, and he liked to play in the afternoon because, on the Tour, he said, 'The late starters were always leading the tournament.'

PGA Tour commissioner Tim Finchem has said that Bolt was 'one of the great personalities to have ever played the game … He was a great showman, and he had a lot to do with the growth of the game because of the interest and excitement he instilled in the fans.'

The Saturday before Thanksgiving 2003, Bolt had a pacemaker fitted. He made it known that he didn't want to talk about club throwing as he was trying to change his image. When asked if at 87 it wasn't a bit late to work on a new reputation, he replied that his surgery might give him a further 87 years. Around the same time, he claimed to have the same interest in sex as he did at 37.

Bolt has continued to take an interest in the modern game and nearly always has insightful views about how it is played and those who play it, but he has always been free with his advice. One great example of this is when he saw Tiger Woods at Riviera in Florida during 1993, a place he knew as a victor and that he loved. Tiger was only 17, but Bolt had heard of him. Studying the young man, Bolt saw him as having a kind of a 'Mule Train' swing, with a bullwhip flip at the top. Bolt took it upon himself to put the left hand of young Woods on top of the club, like Ben Hogan had showed him. Then the old pro stood and watched the lad for a while and marvelled.

But Bolt is not only a teacher. He has a belief that we never stop learning and it was while watching Woods hit a 6-iron 200 yards out of a fairway bunker that he noticed that Tiger kept his lower body very quiet. Bolt copied that move, and he found that he probably caught the ball cleaner out of sand than he had done half a century earlier.

Bolt's greatest regret in golf was that he didn't work harder on his game following his Open win. Winning the Open was all he had ever wanted since boyhood. As a kid he had pretended he was playing for the 'National Open' as his generation called it, but he would go on to appear in that event for real 17 times.

Bolt still plays golf every day (except on the rare occasions when it rains on his Florida home) and continues to shoot from 74 to 76. According to Tommy, when he turned 70, he started setting his goals five years at a time and it has worked so well, in fact, he said that he wished he'd used the same strategy when he was younger. He said that, 'If you can achieve the short-term stuff, you'll do fine in the long run.' He went on to say that, if the day came when he hit his pitching wedge and driver the same distance, that would be the day he'd give up playing.

His allusions to the game have become as famous as his own record and include some hilarious and candid observations: 'The biggest liar in the world is the golfer who claims that he plays the game merely for exercise.'

'There is no better game [than golf] in the world when you are in good company and no worse game when you are in bad company.'

'In golf, driving is a game of free-swinging muscle control, while putting is something like performing eye surgery and using a bread knife for a scalpel.'

'The good chip allows you to whistle while you walk in the dark alleys of golf.'

'Putting allows the touchy golfer two to four opportunities to blow a gasket in the short space of two to 40 feet.'

'Golf is a game where guts, "stick-to-itiveness" and blind devotion will always net you absolutely nothing but an ulcer.'

But he also has a less cynical side: 'You have to try to find the good in everyone and try to like everybody ... I was fortunate enough to win and make money early on, and I'd get a little in my pocket. If some of the caddies couldn't get to the next tournament, I'd help them get there. I've done a little bit of that as quietly as I could.'

The fact that Bolt's golf career was sidetracked a number of times before he ever had a chance to succeed makes his accomplishments more extraordinary. Despite lacking the money to compete on tour, Bolt was one of golf's most determined competitors.

Other than having measles when he was a kid, Bolt has never been sick. He can still read the newspaper without glasses and hear his iron shots hit the green. His memory continues to serve him well, and he keeps his weight down.

Bolt, who has been married to Mary Lou for 45 years (he attributes the longevity of this partnership to the fact that 'we fight fair and try not to go to bed mad at each other'), continues to have his ambitions. Relaxing on a golf course veranda in Florida (his most recent home, having previously lived in Louisiana and Arkansas), wearing the white linen cap that only he, Hogan, Mangrum, Venturi and a few others were allowed to take from his head, he recently stated that he was going to live to be 95 or 100, and that, 'if I don't make it, it will be a total fluke'.

Tommy Bolt has won 29 tournaments. He is also a member of the Florida, Louisiana, Arkansas and Texas Halls of Fame.

PGA TOUR WINS
1951 North & South Open Championship
1952 Los Angeles Open
1953 San Diego Open, Tucson Open
1954 Miami Beach Intl Four-Ball, Insurance City Open, Rubber City Open
1955 Convair-San Diego Open, Tucson Open, St Paul Open
1957 Eastern Open Invitational
1958 Colonial National Invitational, US Open Championship
1960 Memphis Open Invitational
1961 Pensacola Open Invitational

OTHER HONOURS
Best Champions Tour Finishes T3 – 1980 Suntree Senior PGA Tour Classic
Best Champions Tour Finishes 2004 Season Highlights PGA TOUR Playoff Record 3–2

CHAPTER TWENTY

Aftermath

Recovering from two points down after the foursomes, to charge through the singles and win, the Great Britain and Ireland team not only matched what the USA had achieved in 1949 at Ganton, but they actually bettered the Americans' performance in that event by achieving a superior margin of victory. Retrospectively, the whole situation seemed to have transformed in a moment. In the space of an hour, there had been a flurry of results. Bernard Hunt conquered his Wentworth demons and the wins had arrived in a flood, leaving the Americans not knowing what had hit them. There was a tangible feeling of a shockwave having hit the visiting team. The five-point turnaround was astonishingly unpredictable; the USA had been the masters of the singles from the first in the Ryder Cup. A single win (Hawkins) and a half (Mayer) from eight matches amounted to America's worst ever result in the one-on-one competitions.

For Christy O'Connor, 'to lose on the first day was a big setback'. But, just as it seemed that the Americans had their collective tail up, and maybe thought they had it wrapped up safely for yet another two years, the Great Britain and Ireland team tore them apart in the singles to cause the biggest upset of the post-war Ryder Cup series.

At first, Eric Brown (like many others) found the victory difficult to take in. The speed at which the home team had clinched victory left the crowd not quite believing what they were seeing. From a position of strength at lunchtime, Great Britain and Ireland had driven home the advantage in a way that nobody had quite expected. The brilliance of the home team was unquestionable. But what had happened to the Americans? *The Times* golf correspondent suggested a lack of backbone: 'Once they were confronted with the possibility of defeat they collapsed … it was something we do not expect from Americans.'

The USA team may well have been culpable of complacency, as they had dominated the first day. If they had been given some time to refocus, they might have turned things round, but Dai Rees and his men had gone in to lunch on the final day ahead in five matches. There was precious little opportunity for the USA to regroup.

Another factor contributing to the demise of the USA side were the windy conditions out on the course after lunch, which were not suited to low scoring, so the Americans left themselves with too much to do in the remaining 18 holes.

Not that the spectators minded – they cheered every putt sunk by the home side.

Later, Eric Brown was to claim that only 'super-optimists' – among whom he included himself – had fancied that Great Britain and Ireland might win the singles by such a margin and neutralise the USA's lead in the foursomes. Eric suggested that the fact that the British newspapers didn't give the home team the slightest chance of making up the leeway inspired him and his team-mates to surprise their opponents and the golfing world. Brown recalled how some journalists had written off Great Britain and Ireland so arrogantly that he for one was determined to make them eat their words. And how well Eric and his colleagues succeeded in making them do just that.

An abiding memory for the only Scotsman in the 1957 Ryder Cup was the huge overjoyed crowds that swarmed over Lindrick. He was to say that he had 'never seen so many delighted folk on a golf course'.

The jubilant scenes at Lindrick were all the more special for the surprise and speed of the singles victories. Nobody had really expected Great Britain and Ireland to win, and, even if they had, they could not have imagined the scenes that eventually took place.

The crowd stayed on in their thousands to witness Dai Rees collect the trophy and describe the day as 'the proudest moment that I've ever had'. A succession of huge cheers greeted the victorious team as Rees was hoisted on to their shoulders, parading the Cup for the entire crowd to see. It was a day that would live long in the memory of everyone concerned. Determination and teamwork had overcome style and the vast social and economic superiority of American golf. History had also been overcome, never a simple job, but to do it wrestling with the greatest power on earth, sporting, golfing or otherwise, is phenomenal. But, more than anything else, a tiny cohort of men, pulled from the diverse range of environments that make up a little cluster of weather-beaten Northern Atlantic Isles, had stared adversity and the relative poverty of post-war Britain in the face and beaten back these awesome foes with golf clubs.

American anxiety about the deficit of stars in their roster appeared to be vindicated. Once they gained the momentum, the Great Britain and Ireland team simply ran away with the match to win back the trophy that had been a stranger to their shores since 1933.

When asked about his side's capitulation, Jack Burke said he thought that his team had 'overtrained', and that they had come to England too soon and played themselves out in a week of practice. Jackie further concluded that it was a big mistake not to have played more with that little British ball. He said that in the future he was going to suggest that American teams arrive in the UK no earlier than four or five days before the event. He concluded, 'I've known our fellows for a long time, and I've never seen them putt so badly.'

Many years later, Jackie pointed out that the US PGA had 'come through with some nice bonuses' for the players who represented them; Burke told how each of the Americans received a free jacket, two pairs of slacks and some shirts. 'That was it! For the time, it was first-class treatment.'

The USA had agreed to use the smaller British ball and this difference, although slight, did affect some of the Americans.

The defeated captain went on to complain that the pins used were of differing thicknesses and heights, declaring that it was hard to see some from the fairway, while others prevented players from chipping the ball into the hole.

But there were perhaps two major factors that set up the American defeat. The first was their own attitude, letting their professional focus waver on the second day when they seemed to take the matches for granted.

The other big contributor to the US downfall was the clever course preparation. According to Max Faulkner, it was the Great Britain and Ireland players who got the course ready, 'and we made it very English'. The greens weren't watered for three days before the Ryder Cup, and the grass around the green was an inch and a half long. In those days, the Americans didn't know how to play a shot from there.

Christy O'Connor told of how the greens were almost tailor made for the home side: 'Long and detailed preliminary work had gone into preparing the Lindrick course to suit our style of play.'

In the months preceding the match, Lindrick received no special fertiliser or watering treatment so as to avoid the danger of producing lush Americanised conditions. The playing surface was to be allowed to keep its true British links character, and in particular the greens were to be fast and slick. In addition, it was decided by the GB PGA to allow the thick grass behind the green to grow. This was done on the principle that an American's approach shot into a green was by custom and training bold and aimed at the flag, so that any shot that did not sit down on the hard greens would over-pitch and be smothered in the grass (it would also provide the chance of snagging the Americans' balls as they flew through the swift greens).

Max Faulkner remembered a practice session before the Cup started. He was playing the 6th hole with Dai Rees and Ken Bousfield, and Jack Burke was backed in the tall grass, and he had one stab at it. He grabbed the club too tightly, and the ball just jumped in the air and went a foot forward. He did it again, and it jumped a foot forward. Then he picked the ball up and walked away. So the home side saw before official play started that they had an advantage.

But all this should not detract from what really won the Cup for the Great Britain and Ireland team. Rees had instilled a solid teamwork ethic and an aggressive competitive spirit in his men. The home captain decided that, given their form in the foursomes, he would not use Harry Weetman or Max Faulkner in the singles matches. Weetman grumbled to the media and moped throughout most of the second day. But Faulkner chose to take an active role in what was going on. Looking back, he said he thought that a part of him knew that 1957 would be his last Ryder Cup, and all he cared about was winning, whoever played. He recalled, 'If I couldn't do it with a club in my hands, there were other ways.

'It was the highlight for me, to finally break through … We were rather like heroes for a while. It was a great, great cap on my career.'

According to Ken Bousfield, 'Those were the days before

scoreboards out on the course and walkie-talkies. All of us playing out there would have no idea what was happening in the other matches if it wasn't for Max [Faulkner]. He was marvellous.'

And Max seemed to bring good news every time he was seen by his team-mates. He'd get alongside a colleague and tell them: 'Rees is winning.' 'Brown's four up.' 'We've got them on the run, Guv'nor.' 'Go on! You can beat this boy.' Then he'd dash off and come back 10 minutes later with more good news.

For Bousfield, 'We might have won without him, but he was magnificent that day – I'll never forget what he did.'

Bernard Hunt reinforced the spirit of Bousfield's observations about the match: 'I think that we did as well as we did because we played as a team.'

Dai Rees recalled that Faulkner 'took more out of himself on that great day by rushing between matches reporting progress and radiating encouragement than he would have done by playing. I think his enthusiasm alone was worth a point to our side.'

There is little doubt that Faulkner's effort and inspiration played a part in his team's impressive singles performance and departure from tradition. But he was modest about his contribution, and, shortly after the famous triumph, he commented, 'I'm glad I wasn't playing …What, me out there with all those people? I should have been frightened to death.'

It was a bittersweet result for Peter Alliss, but happily the sweetness outlived any disappointment. His own match-play record read played four, lost four. Although he hadn't won a point at Lindrick, he felt that he had played as well as anyone in the team and was very proud to be a member of the winning side: 'The memory has been warm and bright over the many years that were to pass before we found the men who could do it again.'

For all this, Henry Longhurst in *Golf Illustrated* (17 October 1957) seemed to be just a little diffident about the Great Britain and Ireland performance:

It was only this year that the lesson was eventually drummed into a Walker Cup team that you simply cannot beat Americans, broadly speaking, if the whole team are two or three down after the first six holes. Whether it was drummed into the Ryder Cup team by Rees or not, I do not know, but the lesson was there for all to see on both days. On the first it worked for the Americans. On the second for us.

In the foursomes, of the first 10 scores that went up, hole by hole, on the big scoreboard, for the Americans seven were threes and the rest were fours. The first three holes, par 4, 4, 3, measure 400, 358 and 164 yards. The first two American pairs started 3, 3, 3, and the Americans, of course, led by 3–1. In the singles it was the British who were first out of the trap and for the first 80 holes that appeared on the board they were 11 under fours between the six players, while the Americans were eight over. The British won the singles by 6½–1½.

The scoring at the Ryder Cup was magnificently done and was the most up-to-date that I remember. As you may know, I do part of the television commentaries and, stuck up at the top of a 70-foot tower, one is absolutely at the mercy of the people who are responsible for the scores. If the scoring system breaks down, total chaos reigns. Mostly the scoring these days is done by Territorial Army units, who find it useful signals practice and a congenial form of training. The Ryder Cup was no exception, and I hereby lift my hat, on behalf of B.B.C., press and spectators, to the officers and men of the 17/21 Lancers and Sherwood Foresters Yeomanry, who were responsible for the most efficient scoring we have ever had.

A question that keeps recurring to me is 'How can a team of the finest golfers in the world collapse so totally and completely as the Americans did in the singles?' One can understand it in a football team when every man can see the rot setting in around him, or in a cricket team when a succession of quick wickets seems, from the pavilion, to make a bowler unplayable – but how can it happen to men who are separated from each other perhaps by a mile or more? At Lindrick the Saturday was punctuated by roars from all over the course, signifying another putt holed for Britain, but these, while they might upset the actual victim, should hardly have so dramatic an effect on all the others.

I fancy that there were few aspects about their visit which this particular American team enjoyed and there are many changes that simply must be made when this match is held in this country again.

The present point is that, whatever they thought of the affair in general, it did not prevent their winning the foursomes easily enough and almost making a clean sweep of them, and nothing can have happened over Friday night so drastic as to account for total demoralisation in the singles. A strange affair altogether. Let it be added, though, that these thoughts do not fail for a moment to take into account the old golfing truth that in match-play often you play only as well as your opponent lets you.

However, let us forget about them for the moment. The main thing is: WE WON.

Rees and his team had battled hard and well and a congratulatory atmosphere gushed out of the clubhouse at Lindrick. Harry Bradshaw recollected, 'We were drinking champagne until 5 o'clock in the morning … They went mad that day.'

Peter Alliss has made the point that nothing was as big then as it is today. He recalled that everybody got drunk at the dinner, and old journalists, old people, were jumping up and saying a few words and singing and dancing. In contrast the American team looked like men in mourning. Allis recollected, 'We hadn't won since 1933, and the American team looked on in disbelief that they could have lost to this ragtag outfit.'

The US team did not take part in the celebrations, retreating to their hotel at the first opportunity. Tommy Bolt continued to lead the culture of complaint that had now enveloped a section of the defeated side; it seemed nothing had been right for them and not a thing had gone their way: their hotel, the food they had been offered and the partisan

Yorkshire gallery (that Bolt labelled as 'the worst in the world'). For them, things had conspired to rob them of what they had deserved. Notwithstanding the tactful remarks from and on behalf of the USA contingent, the final incivility towards the British PGA hosts came when three of the USA team declined to attend the prize-giving and reception.

Lindrick had seen an intensely competitive confrontation between the Ryder Cup rivals, but it seems there was no lasting acrimony, at least not from the Great Britain and Ireland side. According to Bernard Hunt, 'There was only one American I didn't get on with and that was Dave Miller.'

Hunt had experienced some problems with Sam Snead when the latter employed a bit of gamesmanship in an attempt to upset Hunt but, after the Briton suggested he might 'bury this fucking putter in your head', the Yank desisted from clipping his nails while this particular opponent was putting. Hunt recalled, 'Funnily enough, after that, he never called me Bernard again. From then on, it was always Mr Hunt. But he did send me a nice message on my 70th birthday.'

The Great Britain and Ireland triumph was an especially sweet moment for Dai Rees, who had been waiting 20 years to finally taste victory, being the only link between the 1957 team and the sides of the pre-World War II era. The conquest of the Americans earned Rees almost every sporting accolade possible that year, and it also did much to start the golfing boom in Britain. Soon after the final singles match, he commented, 'It's wonderful. This is the greatest shot in the arm British golf ever had. My team should receive the freedom of nearby Sheffield and all of Britain.'

He later commented, 'They said we would never win, so it was particularly gratifying ... Although the matches were keenly contested, they were played in the best spirit.

'It was the most thrilling day of my life. I was so proud of captaining a winning side that it probably made up for all those disappointments I endured in many British Open Championships.'

The President of the GB PGA, Lord Brabazon, missed the great occasion as he was recovering from an illness, but he wired a message to his captain: 'What a win ... You nearly gave me another heart attack.'

That was quite something from Lord Brabazon of Tara, who was no stranger to excitement. He was born in England on 8 February 1884 and became a member of the House of Lords, but, as a young man, was a keen and pioneering aviator. He was the first person to be licensed in Great Britain as an airplane pilot and, in 1909, Mr Moore-Brabazon, as he was then, won the first all-British competition, sponsored by the *Daily Mail*, for the first machine to fly a circular mile course. In the same year, M. Michelin (of the tyre company fame) offered a prize for a long-distance flight in all-British aviation; this was also won by Mr Moore-Brabazon, who made a flight of 17 miles. In World War I, Brabazon took a leading role in the development of aerial photography.

The most pleasing aspect of the victory for Dai Rees and his team was the way the USA had been subdued; the six American defeats on the second day had been achieved before the final green. The singles had been a massacre. This said, Lindrick was only the third time in 12 meetings that the USA had failed to win the Ryder Cup; it would be a long time before the Americans would taste defeat again – in 1985, close to three decades later.

Most golf enthusiasts and commentators of the time, along with contemporary historians and writers, generally agreed that the Americans lost the Ryder Cup match to better golf, although some individual observers of events thought the visitors were sunk by the amount of 'hospitality' accorded them, especially on the evening before the singles. A few cynics reckoned the amount and length of the speeches made in their honour might have had a detrimental effect.

Dick Mayer blamed his loss of form on the fact that, after winning the Tam O'Shanter, he had been so busy with television and exhibitions that he had not got down to serious tournament play. But also, he said, 'Too much good food and too much wine are bad for golf.'

But, not long after this side's defeat, he said that he would like to play in the British Open Championship 'just to show the folks over here I can play golf'.

There was one drawback in the Great Britain and Ireland victory for the stern Scotsman Eric Brown. Some of the spectators were guilty of describing the British team as 'English', just as some television and radio commentators are liable to speak of England when they should say Britain. According to Brown, this annoyed more people than just himself and he called the habit of referring to Brown of Scotland, Rees of Wales, and Bradshaw and O'Connor of Ireland (half of the singles team) as Englishmen as 'a combination of ignorance and insolence'.

Golf Illustrated (10 October 1957), in its 'Opinion' column, celebrated the good news for British golf:

> We have sustained so many golf defeats over a period of many years that we can be pardoned for feeling so cock-a-hoop after the Ryder Cup win at Lindrick.
>
> Not only was it a memorable victory, but a victory achieved after defeat was staring us in the face. In the singles the British players started off with such determination that the Americans were being knocked for six before they realised it.
>
> For years the familiar spectacle we have had to watch is the Americans being top dogs and our men struggling. This time the position was reversed and let us not deny it was all most pleasant, except, of course, to the visitors. May it be said that except in one instance the Americans accepted the situation in the most sporting manner imaginable.
>
> This Ryder Cup win is the finest shot-in-the-arm British golf has had for years and we thank sincerely the men who administered it, with a special word of praise for Dai Rees, a truly magnificent Captain.

Tom Scott in *Golf Illustrated* (10 October 1957) wrote of 'British Golf's Great Day. Ryder Cup Victory after the Lean Years':

> It is Sunday, October 6th. This morning at 8.30 I left Sheffield for London. The Sheffield–Worksop road was deserted. At points on the Lindrick course were gangs of men picking up the litter and playing were a few

foursomes, pulling their trolleys, enjoying their Sunday morning games. The Captains and the Kings had departed.

Was it only yesterday that we lived through the most exciting, the most memorable hours in the history of British golf? Was it only yesterday that we cheered a result that shook the golfing world and which for the first time in a quarter of a century took British golf to the headlines of the Sunday newspapers?

I can hardly believe it even now and still ask myself the question the US captain, Jackie Burke, asked me after the match with a look on his face as dazed as any knocked-out boxer: 'But what happened?'

After reflection I now know the answer to that and, to continue in the language of boxing, the answer is that the United States team fell for a 'sucker punch'. That is, they received a mortal blow yesterday morning before they had got going.

Why did that take place? Because there was some wind, the greens had become much faster and the Americans could not control the British-size ball, and because they were up against the most determined British opponents an American team has ever faced, a team full of steam that set the pace ...

It was a quiet and thoughtful British party which foregathered in the hotel in Sheffield after the foursomes. We had hoped at least we might share the foursomes, instead we were down 3–1. If the all-over result had been different we should now have been going into the question of that deficit, now it is not necessary. Let us forget it and instead hurry on to live again the day that I warrant no golfer who was present will ever forget.

In years to come, when most of those who were at Lindrick have departed, there will still be rapt attention in a clubhouse bar for some old man who says: 'Yes, that's all very well, but I remember when I was at Lindrick in 1957. That was a day.'

A day indeed!

The moment British golf had waited for some 24 years had come. We had won the Ryder Cup!

What excitement, what cheering! Every British player was loudly applauded as he arrived at the clubhouse. Out there on the course, Alliss, in the best game of the day perhaps, was holding on to Hawkins like a leech. Eventually Alliss was beaten, but it was a defeat with no discredit at all. We felt sorry for Harry Bradshaw and Dick Mayer, battling it out when nothing now mattered, but, like the great competitors they are, they brought their game to the last green to give their match the perfect story book ending, a half in three.

I know our American friends will forgive us if we are making a fuss of our victory. But we have waited so long for it and suffered so many defeats in the interval.

Ladies and gentlemen, I give you the toast: 'The British Ryder Cup team, coupled with the name of their magnificent Captain, David J. Rees.'

RESULTS

Singles

EC Brown (Buchanan Castle) (3 up, 4 up, 3 up)
  beat T Bolt, 4 and 3

RP Mills (Pinner Hill) (4 up, 5 up, 4 up) beat J Burke,
  5 and 3

P Alliss (Parkstone) (1 down, 1 down, all square)
  lost to F Hawkins, 2 and 1

K Bousfield (Coombe Hill) (4 up, 5 up, 6 up) beat
  L Hebert, 4 and 3

DJ Rees (South Herts) (3 up, 4 up, 7 up) beat E Furgol,
  7 and 6

BJ Hunt (Hartsbourne CC) (1 up, 1 up, 5 up) beat
  D Ford, 6 and 5.

C O'Connor (Bundoran) (2 up, all square, 5 up) beat
  D Finsterwald, 7 and 6

H Bradshaw (Portmarnock) (1 up, 1 down, 1 up) halved
  with R Mayer

Foursomes

Alliss and Hunt lost to Ford and Finsterwald, 2 and 1

Bousfield and Rees beat Wall and Hawkins, 3 and 2

Faulkner (Selsey) and Weetman (Selsdon Park) lost to
  Kroll and Burke, 4 and 3

O'Connor and Brown lost to Mayer and Bolt, 7 and 5.

The victory at Lindrick was not to mark a turn of fortune for
the Great Britain and Ireland team in the Ryder Cup. The USA

was not to let what happened in 1957 occur again. The American domination resumed in 1959 at the Eldorado Country Club in Palm Springs. Torturing the visitors with the dry heat of the desert added to the home advantage. Although there was a sense of 'you want to mess with conditions? Try this' at Eldorado, according to Dow Finsterwald, 'I don't recall any "We're going to revenge that loss" sort of thing. I'm not sure that's the spirit those matches should be played in anyway.'

But for Christy O'Connor the Lindrick match did create some negative feelings: 'There was quite a hangover from this game as the Americans took their defeat badly.'

After 1957, the Ryder Cup was not really much of a contest until 1979 when the event became the USA against Europe. The American golfers were getting better, and there were more of them to choose from; the talent pool was smaller within the British Isles.

In the mid-1950s, the idea of making the Ryder Cup an American v British Commonwealth team had been mooted but, following his team's annihilation in 1957, Harry Moffitt, the US PGA president declared, 'After this year's result, we can forget about that for a bit!'

But he was not disturbed by the Ryder Cup result: 'Back home, there has been less interest in the match than there should be ... This year's result is a tonic. Our pros will go all out to try to reverse the conditions in two years. Crowd interest will be greater. Our boys will have a greater incentive than ever to make the team.'

This was a generous response and Moffitt went on to say how the result would prove a wonderful boost to the competition and that the Ryder Cup, whose existence had been under threat, would go on for 'years and years'.

For all this, the words of Dai Rees, spoken to me at Highbury all those years ago, still resonate: 'We won because we really wanted to. Get hold of that feeling and you can probably achieve anything as long as someone else doesn't want it more than you. At Lindrick, something clicked you can't altogether explain and that's what makes it so rare and difficult to achieve. Some people came together and made a thing happen that nobody really thought could happen. That's a miracle, I think. But, then, the best of sport, the best of what humans do, is to make miracles happen. There's nearly always more to people than you think. That's no bad idea to keep in mind. As soon as you think, "They can't do that!" or "We are not good enough", you have probably got it wrong. The key to achievement in this life is not seeing what can't be done, but what can be achieved; blindness to potential is a destructive disease ... being with people while they achieve all they can be is the greatest honour that someone can be given. That's what I got as captain in 1957.'

I have taken Dai's philosophy with me into the rest of my life the best I can. This has meant I have made an effort not to attempt to think that I can 'empower' or 'enable' others. As many of the men who fought it out at Lindrick in 1957 knew, the attempt to do something for others, to 'broaden their experience' or 'make them better' is a futile illusion of the ego; people make themselves out of their own potential; we have it in us to become all we can be. It was that understanding that took the Ryder Lions to the summit of their achievement and it is that legacy that lives on in their example as part of the eternal chronicles of sport that can teach us how to make the most of our shared humanity.

> The triumph of the underdog I've heard say
> Is the lesson that every dog has its day,
> But when the less favoured do all they can
> That is the victory of the common man.
>
> From *The Canning Town Caddie* by Reg Revins